PHILIP ALLAN
LITERATURE GUIDE
FOR GCSE

PHILIP ALLAN

LITERATURE GUIDE

FOR GCSE

THE WOMAN IN BLACK

SUSAN HILL

Margaret Mulheran

With thanks to Jeanette Weatherall for reviewing the manuscript of this book

Philip Allan Updates, an imprint of Hodder Education, an Hachette UK company, Market Place, Deddington, Oxfordshire OX15 0SE

Orders

Bookpoint Ltd, 130 Milton Park, Abingdon, Oxfordshire OX14 4SB
tel: 01235 827827
fax: 01235 400401
e-mail: education@bookpoint.co.uk
Lines are open 9.00 a.m.–5.00 p.m., Monday to Saturday, with a 24-hour message answering service. You can also order through the Philip Allan Updates website: www.philipallan.co.uk

© Margaret Mulheran 2010
ISBN 978-1-4441-1026-5
First printed 2010

Impression number 5 4 3 2
Year 2015 2014 2013 2012

Front cover reproduced by permission of Elisa Lazo de Valdez/Corbis
Page graphic courtesy of Utah Shakespearean Festival

Printed in Spain

Hachette UK's policy is to use papers that are natural, renewable and recyclable products and made from wood grown in sustainable forests. The logging and manufacturing processes are expected to conform to the environmental regulations of the country of origin.

Contents

Getting the most from this book and website

How to use this guide

You may find it useful to read sections of this guide when you need them, rather than reading it from start to finish. For example, you may find it helpful to read the *Context* section before you start reading the novel, or to read the *Plot and structure* section in conjunction with the novel, whether to back up your first reading of the book or to help you revise. The sections relating to assessments will be especially useful in the weeks leading up to the exam.

The following features have been used throughout this guide.

● **How does Hill reveal the characters to us?**

Target your thinking

A list of **introductory questions** to target your thinking is provided at the beginning of each chapter. Look back at these once you have read the chapter and check you have understood each of them before you move on.

Build critical skills

Broaden your thinking about the text by answering the questions in the **Pause for thought** boxes. They are intended to encourage you to consider your own opinions in order to develop your skills of criticism and analysis.

Pause for thought

Grade-boosting advice

Pay particular attention to the **Grade booster** boxes. Students with a firm grasp of these ideas are likely to be aiming for the top grades.

Grade **booster**

PHILIP ALLAN LITERATURE GUIDE **FOR GCSE**

Key quotations are highlighted for you, and you may wish to use them as evidence in your examination answers. Page references are given for the Vintage edition of the text (ISBN 978-0-099-51164-9).

Key quotation

At my feet stood a sturdy little terrier with a rough brindle coat and bright eyes.

(p. 100, l. 24)

Be exam-ready

The **Grade focus** sections explain how you may be assessed and distinguish between higher and foundation responses.

Grade *focus*

Get the top grades

Use the **Text focus** boxes to practise evaluating the text in detail and looking for evidence to support your understanding.

Text **focus**

Develop evaluation skills

Review your learning

Test your knowledge

Use the **Review your learning** sections to test your knowledge after you have read each chapter. Answers to the questions are provided in the final section of the guide.

 Don't forget to go online for even more free revision activities and self-tests: **www.philipallan.co.uk/literatureguidesonline**

How to approach the text

Above all, a novel is written to be enjoyed. The author's purpose is to entertain and the skill of a writer, particularly of a ghost story, is to grip readers and keep them enthralled right to the end.

In order to enjoy *The Woman in Black,* you need to get to know the characters and events so you can keep track of the plot. This guide will help you do this, but it is important to jot down your own ideas and feelings as you read. If you have your own copy, it might be helpful to annotate it, although if it belongs to your school or college you will not be allowed to do this. However, post-it notes are a useful aid to learning and you can use them to make notes about the main events and who is involved. Leave the post-its in your book until just before your exam because they will help your revision and help you to understand the overall structure.

In order to gain the best possible grade in the exam, you need to have studied *The Woman in Black* in great detail. This involves knowing a lot more than the plot. In the *Tackling the exam* section of this guide we will look more closely at the Assessment Objectives (AOs). These are 'examiner speak' for what an examiner is looking for in your answer.

To prepare your mind for studying literature, there are a few things you should think about as you begin the novel. Remember it is a ghost story, so take particular note of the **setting** (when and where the action takes place) and how this influences your feelings as the events unfold. You also need to understand the characters and the times in which they lived. Notice what they say and do and what other characters say about them. Think about their feelings and attitudes and any clues you think the author gives us about what is going to happen.

As you read, you will begin to consider the point of the story and the themes Susan Hill is exploring. She is still alive and well and has her own website (**www.susan-hill.com**), which is a distinct advantage as you can do some research of your own. (Just search for 'Susan Hill' and you will find a lot of information.) Discuss your ideas with your fellow students and become familiar with the conventions of a traditional ghost story. These are like the ingredients of a recipe. What does a ghost story need to contain? How does the author present the mix in the most effective way?

All these aspects of *The Woman in Black* are dealt with in this guide but remember you, the reader, are the most important element in this story. What effect does the novel have on you? What are your thoughts and feelings? To gain an A* in this exam, the examiner is looking for sophisticated interpretation, backed up with details from the text. This means you must have confidence in your own reactions to the novel and be able to express your ideas and feelings clearly.

Context

The 'context' of a novel means the circumstances in which it was written: the social, historical and literary factors that influenced what the author wrote. *The Woman in Black* is a novel in which the social context is important. It is a ghost story that spans the latter half of the nineteenth century and the first half of the twentieth century when the role of women was far more restricted than it is now.

Comparison with modern times

Although you will not earn marks directly in the GCSE examination for being able to compare the social/historical context of *The Woman in Black* with modern times, knowledge of this will help you understand the novel more fully. The period in which the novel is set is vague but the main events occur some time at the beginning of the twentieth century. Although cars had been invented, they were used exclusively by rich people (e.g. Samuel Daily). The pony and trap was commonplace. Similarly, telephones were a relatively new invention and were treated with suspicion. Note that Mr Bentley did not like using them and the young Kipps communicated with his fiancée, Stella, by letter.

However, the most important aspect of *The Woman in Black*, which it is essential to understand, is the position of women in society and the strict Christian moral code of the time. Sex outside marriage was unacceptable and indeed considered both sinful and shameful. Remember, there was no reliable contraception until the introduction of 'the pill' in the 1960s. Illegitimate children (children whose parents were not married at the time of their birth) had no inheritance rights and were second-class citizens. For many, it was a social stigma they carried through life. The idea of an unmarried couple either living together or having children was impossible to imagine at the time. If a young girl became pregnant, she was usually sent far away to relatives or family friends to have the baby and was returned to the family once the confinement was over, having been forced to put the baby up for adoption. Even then, the future of the

Homerby/Crythin Gifford is somewhere between Holy Island and the Essex Marshes. Arthur Kipps' journey takes him from London, King's Cross to Crewe and then over to the east coast, sometime in November between 1900 and 1914

Edinburgh

Holy Island

Glasgow

North Sea

Newcastle upon Tyne

Belfast

Darlington

ISLE OF MAN

Leeds

Hull

Irish Sea

Liverpool

Manchester

Dublin

Crewe

Nottingham

Norwich

Birmingham

Leicester

Luton

Ipswich

Swindon

London

ESSEX MARSHES

Cardiff

Bristol

Reading

Southend-on-Sea

Southampton

Exeter

girl was bleak and her marriage chances were slim. She would have been viewed as wicked or mentally ill and the treatment of such people at the time was very similar. Some women were committed to lunatic asylums and forgotten about, such was the shame they were believed to have brought on their families. There was no way out for them. Abortion was against the law until the late 1960s and the risks of 'back-street' (illegal) abortions were life threatening.

It was in these circumstances that Jennet Humfrye brought Nathaniel Pierston into the world. Although she was fortunate (after a struggle) to have her baby adopted by her sister and to have been allowed to see him, it is hardly surprising that revenge took over her whole being both after his death and into eternity. In fact, it could be said that being allowed to see him made her plight even worse. We are told that as she bonded with him, his relationship with Alice Drablow, his adoptive mother, weakened. Some people in the village believed Jennet planned to take him away. If that was the case, it meant that as a result of his death she had been forcibly parted from him a second time, which was too much for her to bear.

Susan Hill intended to write a full-length ghost story, which is unusual as they are most commonly written in novella or short-story form. She first became interested in ghost stories when she played a part in the dramatised version of Dickens' *A Christmas Carol*, and she felt that the form of the classic ghost story was being neglected due to the rise in popularity of the horror genre. Susan Hill's inspiration for the novel came from reading *The Turn of the Screw* by Henry James.

The Woman in Black is set somewhere on the east coast of England which is famous for its salt marshes and sea mists, although the actual ghost story begins during 'a London Particular', or a 'pea-souper' — the popular name for the thick fogs made up of greenish yellow smoke and mist which used to plague all the major industrial cities before the government introduced the Clean Air Act in 1956.

Susan Hill

Susan Hill was born in Scarborough, North Yorkshire, in 1942 and attended Scarborough Convent School until she was 16. In 1958 the family moved to Coventry where she attended Barr's Hill Girls' Grammar School and from there she went on to read English at King's College, London. As a student, she wrote her first novel, *The Enclosure*, which was published by Hutchinson in 1961. She also had her second novel, *Do Me a Favour*, published while she was at university after which she worked as a journalist on a Coventry local newspaper for five years.

Her best-known novel, *I'm the King of the Castle*, was published in 1970 and won the Somerset Maugham Award. *The Woman in Black* was published in 1983 and adapted for stage by Stephen Mallatratt in 1988 (the play is still running in the West End). This happened by chance: Mallatratt picked up her book at the airport while on holiday at a time when he was looking for a play to stage. It posed several problems for him as there are scenes in the book which are not easily adapted to the

TopFoto

The Actor (Ben Port) and Kipps (Sean Baker) in Stephen Mallatratt's production at the Fortune Theatre, London

stage, for instance the vast landscape of the marshes and the important parts played by animals. He got round this by using Arthur Kipps as narrator, with Kipps employing an actor who encourages him to present his story as a play. As they immerse themselves in the task, events take a supernatural turn.

Although the script stays true to the original plot, there are some changes. For instance, Esmé and her family do not feature at all. The most outstanding difference is the ghostly dimension added by Mallatratt, which works superbly as drama. The woman in black appears on stage in appropriate places throughout the narrative. Kipps is unaware of this but the actor portraying him believes that Kipps has actually arranged for someone else to play her part. It slowly dawns on the audience that they are becoming part of the narrative and are not merely onlookers.

It took Susan Hill six weeks to write the book. Initially, she wrote a preface to the text in the voice of Oliver Ainley, Kipps' step-son who tells of how he found Kipps' untouched manuscript after Kipps' death in old age and how deeply it had affected the whole family. This was not included in the published version but you can read it in *Susan Hill: The Essential Guide* by Margaret Reynolds and Jonathan Noakes published by Vintage (ISBN 978-0-0-9954-239-1).

Review your learning

(Answers given on p. 84)

1 Why is the social/historical context particularly important in *The Woman in Black*?

2 How were women treated in the middle of the nineteenth century?

3 Which texts inspired Susan Hill to write *The Woman in Black*?

4 What is Susan Hill's most famous novel?

5 How long did it take Susan Hill to write *The Woman in Black*?

6 Who adapted the novel for the West End stage?

7 What problems did *The Woman in Black* pose for staging?

8 How did Mallatratt overcome these problems?

 More interactive questions and answers online.

Plot and structure

- What are the main events of the novel?
- How do these events unfold chapter by chapter?
- How does Hill create a structure in these events?

Plot

Susan Hill separates the novel into chapters each with its own heading. Although they are not numbered in the text, it would be helpful to pencil in the numbers for ease of reference. The novel is written in the first person, the story being told by Arthur Kipps in his middle age.

Chapter 1: Christmas Eve

- A peaceful fireside family Christmas Eve at Monk's Piece. The Kipps' family home is described.
- Arthur Kipps (the narrator) a retired solicitor, steps outside to describe the house's setting and to reminisce.
- Kipps describes how several years ago he discovered Monk's Piece and felt compelled to buy it.
- Mr Bentley, a retired solicitor and Arthur's former employer and late partner, is introduced.
- Arthur's wife and step-family are introduced to establish a happy domestic scene and a springboard from which to tell the main story.
- This family plays no part in subsequent chapters.
- Arthur is invited by Edmund to contribute a ghost story which stirs up suppressed emotions. Although he declines, he resolves to write down his story.
- Arthur remembers lines from Shakespeare's *Hamlet* where Marcellus speaks to Horatio and Barnardo after seeing the ghost of Hamlet's father.
- Comforted by this verse, Kipps returns to the house to join in the Christmas activities.

Pause for thought

These characters are introduced purely to provide a context for Kipps' ghost story. In what ways do you think they behave like a typical family?

In 'Christmas Eve', Susan Hill prepares her readers for a traditional ghost story. Arthur Kipps, his wife Esmé and her four grown children share Christmas Eve together. Invited to contribute a ghost story to the evening's entertainment, terrifying memories of a supernatural experience are evoked and Arthur resolves to exorcise his ghost by writing his story in the New Year.

In the opening paragraph, Hill describes an idyllic family Christmas. After dinner, as Arthur's family gather around the hearth, he steps out to enjoy the evening air. In his descriptions of the seasonal settings we learn something of his state of mind.

> **Key quotation**
>
> **My spirits have for many years now been excessively affected by the ways of the weather...**
>
> (p. 10, l. 7)

He continues to say how he is prone to 'gloom and lethargy' and is unable to enjoy life as though this is somehow connected with his past. He tells the reader how he discovered Monk's Piece, an isolated house on a hill, while travelling with Mr Bentley, his former employer and mentor, and felt a powerful force compelling him to purchase it.

Hill paints a very clear picture of Arthur's background. He was a widower at the age of 23 and at 35 he married Esmé Ainley and they moved into Monk's Piece with her four children: Isobel, aged ten; Oliver, five; William, four; and one-year-old Edmund.

> **Pause for thought**
>
> Arthur has a particular affinity with the youngest, Edmund, possibly because he is the closest in age to his own son whom we learn about later in the story.

The Christmas Eve of the first chapter takes place 14 years later when all the family is gathered together with the addition of Isobel's husband: 'the calm and level-headed Aubrey Pearce' and their three infant sons who are in bed.

On returning indoors, Arthur discovers his family is upholding the Christmas tradition of telling ghost stories by the fireside. At first the atmosphere is jolly and good humoured as the young men exploit the conventions of ghost stories in a ridiculous fashion but Arthur becomes increasingly remote from the fun and begins to panic. When invited to make his contribution, he leaves the room abruptly and escapes to the scrub land beyond the house where he contemplates telling his own ghost story.

> **Key quotation**
>
> **...a true story, a story of haunting and evil, fear and confusion, horror and tragedy.**
>
> (p. 21, l. 28)

Grade *booster*

The author's use of language: Susan Hill uses a pattern of three adjectival phrases effectively here to build tension and excitement. Grade C candidates would recognise such language features and add a general comment on the fact they increase the tension. A and A* candidates would analyse how the words are put together, the sounds they make and how they form a rhythm in the sentence.

Text focus

Look carefully at 'Christmas Eve' from page 18, line 28 beginning, 'The lonely country house...' to the end of page 20. Read it several times.

- The Ainley boys are setting the scene for their firelight ghost story session which stimulates Arthur Kipps' resolve to write in the New Year about his ghostly encounter in order to purge the ghost for good. The atmosphere is giddy. The family is high spirited and excited as they take part in the festive tradition. Each of the boys is trying to out-do the other two. Everyone is enjoying themselves apart from Kipps.
- Susan Hill is deliberately creating a light-hearted atmosphere. She shows how human beings deal with phenomena they cannot explain. One way is to ridicule and exaggerate the things that frighten us, particularly when we are young. We learn later that as a young man, Kipps was adamant that he did not believe in ghosts.
- When Edmund presses Kipps to take his turn to tell a ghost story he tries to refuse light-heartedly. He doesn't know what to say other than that he has no story to tell. The truth, however, is the opposite. He is the only one who actually does have a true story too terrible to tell.
- This episode paves the way for the remainder of the novel. This happy domestic scene foreshadows the terrible tale of *The Woman in Black*.
- After the first chapter, these characters (except for Kipps) play no further part in the narrative.
- List the main features of ghost stories that you can identify from this passage.
- Trace Kipps' feelings, step-by-step through this passage then write a paragraph showing what you have learned about his character.

Pause for thought

Christmas is a time for celebrating family life and the fact that Arthur cannot join in the fun suggests that something sinister has disturbed him. Can you think of a Christmas in your life when something was worrying you and you did not feel like joining in the fun? How did you deal with your feelings?

Once away from the family, Arthur calms down but realises he must tell his ghost story not for entertainment but to exorcise his demon. Comforted by a learned quotation from *Hamlet* which describes how in the sacred season of Christmas, ghosts and malevolent spirits dare not walk the earth, he returns home determined to enjoy Christmas and to write his true story in the New Year.

Review your learning

(Answers given on p. 84)
1. What do you learn about Mr Bentley in this chapter?
2. Describe Monk's Piece and its setting.
3. What do you learn from this chapter about Arthur Kipps' state of mind?

More interactive questions and answers online.

Grade *booster*

Foreshadowing is a technique used by authors to suggest events to come, for example page 22, line 27 onwards 'I was the one who had been haunted and who had suffered — not the only one, no, but surely, I thought the only one left alive,...'. To attain the top grades, use examples of foreshadowing (relevant to the question) in your answer.

Chapter 2: A London Particular

- A description of a London fog.
- Description of hell (pp. 26–27). Arthur's sense of foreboding, his sixth sense or telepathic intuition.
- Mr Bentley's clerk, Tomes, is introduced.
- Arthur sets off on his journey to Crythin Gifford.
- We learn that Arthur was engaged to Stella.

The time is November, 26 years before the Christmas Eve of Chapter 1. Arthur's own true ghost story begins. Like Chapter 1, Chapter 2 begins with a description of the weather — a pea-souper or a 'London Particular'. 'London Particular' is the name of a recipe for pea soup which is also used as a colloquial term for a thick fog. Hill uses pathetic fallacy to introduce foreboding or a sixth sense.

Arthur Kipps at the age of 23 is being sent by his employer to attend the funeral of Mrs Alice Drablow, who died aged 87, to sort out her papers and to return with them to London. This involves a journey through the fog, by cab, to King's Cross station, catching a steam locomotive to Crewe, then on to Homerby to change once more for Crythin Gifford, a fictitious town on the east coast salt marshes.

An air of mystery is built up around Alice Drablow of Eel Marsh House. The pace of the story is slowed down by the introduction of dialogue which feeds the reader simple facts through Arthur's questioning of Mr Bentley. Mr Bentley adds mystery to the story by seeming deliberately cagey.

Pause for thought

'Pathetic fallacy' is a term coined by the great writer John Ruskin to describe attributing human feelings to the weather and the natural world. It is often used to foreshadow a terrible event or act, as an omen does in classical writing. Can you find an example of this in another text you have studied — the Shakespeare text perhaps?

Pause for thought

The presence of steam locomotives (another element of a traditional ghost story) is introduced. They were seen as supernatural monsters that carved up the countryside and killed sheep and cattle at will. They are common in many of Dickens' ghost stories, which inspired Susan Hill. Have you ever thought how 'the ghost train' got its name? Search on the internet to find out.

Dan Kremer and James
Stellos in the Utah
Shakespearean Festival's
2009 production of *The
Woman in Black* (photo by
Karl Hugh)

Utah Shakespearean Festival

Text focus

Read the dialogue (the conversation) between
Kipps and Mr Bentley, from pages 28–31 up to 'I
got up' (l. 28).

● This is the first time that Kipps hears of Alice
Drablow and her affairs. He is quite pleased
to be given an interesting task instead of 'dull
details of the conveyance of property leases'.
Kipps is a young man, impatient to progress in
his career and marry his fiancée.

● Susan Hill is deliberately creating an air of
mystery around Alice Drablow. Notice the short,
clipped and sometimes incomplete sentences,
the use of pauses and how Kipps sometimes
repeats Bentley's words to indicate surprise.
Notice the pattern of Bentley's speech, the
frequent pauses and the seemingly pointless
rhetorical questions.

● Gout is a very painful disease where the blood
circulation does not extend to the toes and
nerve endings become inflamed. In Victorian
times it was believed to be brought on by
drinking too much alcohol and eating too
much rich food. However, in more recent times
this has been found not to be the case. Indeed,
Mr Bentley was 'abstemious'. This means he
was a very moderate, clean-living man who
was not at all self-indulgent.

● When Kipps asks Bentley if Alice Drablow
had children he pauses for a long time before
he replies in the negative. Remember this as
it becomes particularly significant later in the
story. Notice how the church bell tolls before
he answers. This sound is traditionally used
to signify that someone has died or is about
to die.

● Do you think Mr Bentley is being deliberately
vague or is he just old?

● In what ways does Mr Bentley appear to be an
eccentric character?

● Sum up what Kipps learns from this conversation.

Alice Drablow was widowed young and was childless. She had lived in a very remote house that was regularly cut off from the mainland by incoming tides. She owned a modest amount of property and the usual trusts and investments for a lady of her social class at that time (early 1900s). She is described as 'a rum 'un' and was apparently friendless.

Arthur is pleased to be given more responsibility as he is entrusted with important business. He leaves the chambers having written a note to his fiancée, Stella, saying he will be away for a few days.

Review your learning

(Answers given on p. 85)

1 What is 'a London Particular' and how does it get its name?
2 What do you learn about Kipps' occupation in this chapter?
3 Who is Alice Drablow and what is Kipps' business with her?
4 Pick out references to the supernatural in this chapter.
5 How does Hill use similes to create vivid images in the reader's mind?

More interactive questions and answers online.

Grade *booster*

To attain the highest grades you must show appreciation and consideration of the writer's use of language, for example the significance of Tomes — the clerk's name suggests he spends a great deal of time in small, cupboard-type rooms with big, heavy law books. Foundation candidates may possibly mention this but higher candidates would be expected to include such details in the context of explaining how Susan Hill creates mystery and suspense.

Chapter 3: The Journey North

- The journey by steam locomotives from King's Cross to Crewe and across to the fictional town of Homerby near the east coast.
- Again, the weather is emphasised.
- The introduction of Mr Samuel Daily.
- Note the curious place names and the author's description of sounds.

Chapter 3 describes Arthur's journey north from King's Cross, London, changing trains at Crewe and Homerby. Homerby is a fictitious town east of Crewe (pp. 34–35).

Pause for thought

Note the name of the tunnel: Gapemouth. Does Susan Hill give any other place names that describe themselves in the novel?

He learns through a fellow traveller from Homerby that he has not escaped the mist and fog, as sea frets or mists are common around their destination. His companion notices the name 'Drablow' on Arthur's envelope and after introducing himself as Samuel Daily, whose business is real estate, the conversation becomes more amicable and Arthur accepts a lift in Daily's car to the Gifford Arms.

Key quotation

We tuck ourselves in with our backs to the wind, and carry on with our business.

(p. 39, l. 7)

Text focus

Read the last two paragraphs of the third chapter. Look at the Key quotation on this page relating to Crythin Gifford, 'We tuck ourselves in…'.

- The people of Crythin Gifford appear to be surrounded by a hostile environment and, like animals, they seek to protect themselves from outsiders. What clues does this give you about how the people will respond to a naïve, confident young lawyer from London prying into their affairs?
- This is a very short chapter. All that happens is that Kipps travels by train to Homerby and meets Samuel Daily. Susan Hill uses this chapter to consolidate the air of mystery and suspense. By now it should be clear to the reader that Crythin Gifford hides the secret of terrible events. Samuel Daily silently confirms some of what Mr Bentley began. Alice Drablow died friendless, her housekeeper was dead and her relatives escaped to South Africa 40 years previously. There is likely to be no-one at her funeral except business acquaintances. There will be nobody to mourn her passing.

Review your learning

(Answers given on p. 85)

1 Describe Samuel Daily.
2 What evidence is there in this chapter that Arthur Kipps is a fairly young, inexperienced man?
3 What are sea frets?
4 How do the noises of the train add to the feelings of fear and foreboding?
5 The name of the locomotive was 'The Sir Bedivere'. What does the name suggest?

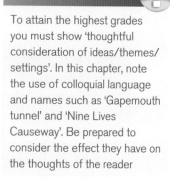

Grade **booster**

To attain the highest grades you must show 'thoughtful consideration of ideas/themes/ settings'. In this chapter, note the use of colloquial language and names such as 'Gapemouth tunnel' and 'Nine Lives Causeway'. Be prepared to consider the effect they have on the thoughts of the reader

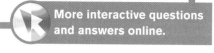
More interactive questions and answers online.

Chapter 4: The Funeral of Mrs Drablow

- The comfort of the Griffin Arms.
- The strange reaction of the landlord when he learns of Kipps' business in Crythin Gifford.
- We are introduced to Mr Jerome, the land agent who dealt with Alice Drablow's property.
- The funeral.
- The appearance of the woman in black.
- Mr Jerome's alarm.
- Kipps returns to the Gifford Arms.
- Mr Daily's successful day at the auction.
- Kipps learns that there will be no buyers for Eel Marsh House.

Having arrived at Crythin Gifford and settled in comfortably at the homely Gifford Arms, Arthur looks forward to a substantial, home-cooked supper. He writes a note to Stella and begins to ponder their future together now his career is taking off. He begins to speculate on where they might live and whether he should ask for a pay-rise.

After supper and half a bottle of claret, he bids goodnight to the landlord who asks if he intends to participate in the auction to be held in the public bar the following day. When Arthur tells the landlord of his intention to attend the funeral of Alice Drablow he detects 'Alarm...?' or 'Suspicion?' Whatever the emotion, the landlord's manner definitely becomes less friendly. Arthur's suspicions begin to be aroused.

Grade *booster*

In the middle of page 43 the chronology of the narrative is interrupted as Arthur, the storyteller, reflects upon not just the events of the day but his feelings about the events at the time. He returns to the present and affirms his happiness in later life, married to Esmé. This adds depth to the plot and is a device that Susan Hill uses effectively to build tension and suspense. Higher candidates will be expected to comment on this when writing about structure and the skill with which Susan Hill successfully merges the past and the present to give the reader insight into the effects of what is about to happen.

After the best night's sleep and in contrast to the gloom and foreboding of the day before, the day of the funeral dawns with a clear blue sky, warm, autumn sunshine and the noisy, bustling, cheerful atmosphere of market day. Kipps feels a sense of comfort and safety and begins to understand Daily's description of Crythin Gifford.

Key quotation

Nonetheless, I had been left in no doubt that there was some significance in what had been left *uns*aid.

(p. 43, l. 12)

Key quotation

Indeed, even now in later life, though I have been as happy and at peace in my home at Monk's Piece, and with my dear wife Esmé, as any man may hope to be, and even though I thank God every night that it is all over, all long past and will not, *cannot* come again...

(p. 44, l. 37)

Pause for thought

Notice how Hill personifies the town to create a sense of snugness and safety.

Key quotation

We tuck ourselves in with our backs to the wind...

(p. 39, l. 7)

Key quotation

...it seemed poignant that a woman, who was perhaps only a short time away from her own death, should drag herself to the funeral of another.

(p. 49, l. 16)

Kipps meets Mr Jerome, Alice Drablow's agent, who is to accompany him to the funeral. Once more he doesn't feel his questions regarding the Drablow family and affairs are being answered fully and honestly. Kipps and Jerome are the only mourners at her funeral until, towards the end, Kipps notices a woman in black at the back of the church who slips away to stand some yards from the graveside waiting for the coffin to be lowered.

Text focus

Look carefully at the third paragraph on page 48 beginning 'However, towards the end of it...'.

- Kipps has arrived at the church with Mr Jerome for Alice Drablow's funeral. He remarks on the sadness of the occasion particularly when the only mourners are himself (who never met the deceased), the vicar and the funeral director's employees. He believes there to be no friends or family present to pay their respects or to mourn the passing of a loved one; that is until he glimpses a woman in black.
- Ironically, he is touched by the sight of the woman in black as she appears so ill. This is the first time the ghost appears and we later learn that she is a malevolent presence intent on doing harm, not as Kipps mistakenly assumes, a friend of the deceased.
- Notice how long this paragraph is, almost a page and a half. Susan Hill presents the ghost through the eyes of Kipps in such fine detail that the reader has almost a photographic image of her.
- Pick out the clues the writer gives to suggest that (although Kipps doesn't realise it) the woman in black is a supernatural presence.
- The phrase 'a spectre at the feast' suggests the spirit of someone looking over your shoulder spoiling your enjoyment of something. It was market day in Crythin Gifford; the town was bustling and colourful. Kipps felt out of place in his funeral clothes.

The reaction of Mr Jerome, when Kipps shows concern for the young woman's wellbeing, is one of pure fear. He denies having seen her and he wishes to leave the churchyard as quickly as possible.

Back at the Gifford Arms, Jerome tells Kipps that a Mr Keckwick will assist him in avoiding the tides on his journey to Eel Marsh House. In conversation with the landlord about the day's land auction, he learns that Samuel Daily has been the successful buyer. It turns out that he is a very rich landowner in these parts and is unpopular because of it, but according to one of the local farmers, not even he would consider buying Alice Drablow's estate. Once more, when Kipps asks why, he is shunned.

Pause for thought

There appears to be a conspiracy of silence surrounding Alice Drablow's affairs.

Review your learning

(Answers given on pp. 85–86)

1. In the early twentieth century, what did Londoners believe about people in the more remote parts of the country?
2. Who was Mr Jerome and what was his business?
3. Describe the appearance of the woman in black.
4. Why was Kipps 'both curious and a little irritated' by the landlord's manner?
5. What did Kipps glean about the inhabitants from the layout of the town?

 More interactive questions and answers online.

Grade *booster*

On page 44, Susan Hill brings the story back to the present. Be prepared to explain how this is used to foreshadow later events in Kipps' story. Higher candidates are expected to show depth of personal response here and be able to unpick the quotation 'innocence, once lost, is lost forever' (p. 44, l. 10).

Chapter 5: Across the Causeway

- Keckwick arrives in a pony and trap to take Kipps to Eel Marsh House.
- We see the magnificent landscape and wildlife as they cross the causeway.
- Eel Marsh House and its surroundings are described.
- Kipps sees the woman in black again.
- Seriously shaken, Kipps returns to the house.
- Kipps decides to set off on foot back to Crythin Griffin intending to intercept Keckwick.

Keckwick arrives in a shabby pony and trap to take Kipps to Eel Marsh House. As they pass the graveyard, Kipps remembers 'the ill-looking, solitary young woman' (p. 58, l. 19).

Hill likens the landscape to Dutch paintings and the East Anglian Fens. Kipps is impressed by the beauty of the 'absolutely flat countryside' and 'the sudden, harsh, weird cries from birds near and far' (p. 59, l. 33).

Grade *booster*

Susan Hill uses the weather to bring out the beauty of Kipps' surroundings on the journey to Eel Marsh House. Be prepared to comment on the details of the setting and the effect it has on Kipps' state of mind.

After about three miles, they reach the Nine Lives Causeway, a sandy path leading to Eel Marsh House, 'a tall, gaunt house of grey stone' (p. 60, l. 23) standing on a little island amid scrub land and a field which included the ruins of an old monastery. Hill uses the effect of sound throughout this chapter to create the sense of splendour and isolation.

Having arrived at the house, Kipps suggests to the silent Keckwick that he intends to return with him to the Gifford Arms later that afternoon and to return the following day with overnight provisions as he intends to sleep at the house. Keckwick makes no comment and departs. Kipps begins to soak in the atmosphere of his surroundings and romanticises about living in such a house with Stella.

Before entering the house he decides to explore the ruined monastery and is alarmed when he disturbs a bird.

Passing through the stone arches, he enters a small burial ground and sees the woman in black once more. He stares at her and sees an expression of 'a desperate, yearning malevolence' (p. 65, l. 16) as though she were seeking something she wanted. It was a look of 'purest evil and hatred and loathing' (p. 65, l. 20). Kipps was petrified but the woman slipped behind a gravestone and disappeared. His terror then turned to anger and he decided to pursue her but she eluded him.

At this point, he ran back to the house in a state of nervous anxiety resolving to get to the bottom of the mystery before completing his business at Eel Marsh House.

Up to this point Kipps sees himself as a 'rational, sensible' young man (p. 67, l. 26) but, after his second encounter with the woman in black, he begins to accept the possibility she may be a ghost and that the place is haunted. He asserts, 'I did not believe in ghosts' (p. 67, l. 24).

Pause for thought

A cat supposedly has nine lives. Could this suggest that the causeway is linked with death?

Pause for thought

What words does Susan Hill use to suggest the sounds and how do they help create atmosphere?

Key quotation

...an ugly satanic-looking thing...

(p. 63, l. 22)

Pause for thought

This time, a malevolent bird seems to herald the reappearance of the woman in black. What effect does this have on Kipps? Wandering spirits were thought to have some unfinished business on earth. How does this link to the quotation from Hamlet in the first chapter (p. 23)?

Text focus

Study the passage from the second complete paragraph on page 67 beginning 'I did not believe in ghosts' up to the repetition of 'I did not believe in ghosts' on page 68.

- The young, innocent, confident, carefree, rational, sensible Kipps at last faces what he believed to be impossible — the woman in black is indeed a ghost. However she is not as Kipps imagined a traditional ghost to be.
- Look back at page 19 and think how she may differ from tradition.
- Consider the effect of this realisation on Kipps.
- How do you think this may affect what he does from this point onwards in the story?
- The ghost is clearly haunting Kipps. What motive could she possibly have?

On entering the house, Kipps proceeds to explore each of the ground floor rooms. He finds nothing remarkable and he is overcome by the feeling of solitude. He decides 'a good brisk walk' back to the Gifford Arms would strengthen his spirits. He sets off towards the Nine Lives Causeway.

James Stellos and Katie Wackowski in the Utah Shakespearean Festival's 2009 production of *The Woman in Black* (photo by Karl Hugh)

Utah Shakespearean Festival

Review your learning

(Answers given on p. 86)

1. Draw a diagram of Eel Marsh House and its surroundings as accurately as you can.

2. Explain how the second appearance of the woman in black is more frightening than her appearance in Chapter 4.

3. Find several references to sound in this chapter and explain their effect on the reader.

4. 'I did not believe in ghosts' repeats Arthur Kipps on pages 67 and 68. How does Susan Hill suggest the woman in black is a ghost?

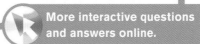

More interactive questions and answers online.

Chapter 6: The Sound of a Pony and Trap

- A sea fret descends and Kipps decides to return to the safety of the house.
- He hears a cry of a child and the sinking of a pony and trap in the quicksand. He assumes they are with Keckwick.
- Kipps is helpless and once more returns to the house, terrified.
- Fortified by brandy, he explores the house and finds a locked door with no key hole.
- He falls asleep on a sofa and is awakened by Keckwick at 2 a.m.
- They return to the Griffin Arms where Kipps relives the nightmare, dreaming of the woman in black.

Some way along the causeway, Kipps realises that the visibility is diminishing as he begins to feel 'a thick, damp, sea-mist' descending (p. 73, l. 11). He realises his safest plan of action would be to return to the house. 'The walk back was a nightmare' (p. 73, l. 34). In the distance he hears the sound of a pony and trap and assumes it is Keckwick coming to collect him. To his alarm, he hears a child screaming and the sound of a pony and trap being sucked into the marshes. He yells out and runs to help but realises in time that the most sensible thing would be to return to the house and switch on all the lights so it might act as a beacon. He manages to do this but is overcome by hopelessness and the enormity and inevitability of what has just occurred.

Having been restored to some sort of calm, he wanders through the upper storeys of the house and discovers a locked door on the second floor. It has no key hole and no exterior bolt. In anger, Kipps kicks it and rattles the handle but it doesn't budge. He returns downstairs and after consuming more brandy, falls asleep on the plush-covered sofa.

Kipps is woken by the ringing of a bell. It is 2 a.m. and Keckwick has returned to fetch him. The mist has cleared and the tide has gone out. Kipps' first thought is that Keckwick has somehow escaped and he voices the question. He quickly realises how impossible that is and wonders who else would be on the causeway and where might they be going.

Although Keckwick appears to be aware that Kipps is traumatised, his manner tells Kipps he does not want any discussion.

On the journey back to the inn, Kipps accepts that the woman in black is a ghost and that in all likelihood the sinking of the pony and trap and the drowning of the child was a ghostly incident also.

Once in the safety of his bed, Kipps thinks about the kindnesses of both the landlord and Keckwick on his return in the middle of the night, but he detects a barrier between him and them, designed to put him off asking any questions. He decides to return to London. Once asleep, he relives the nightmare of the previous afternoon.

Pause for thought

The number of people being enigmatic (mysterious) is increasing: first, the landlord, then Jerome followed by the farmer and now Keckwick. What is going on in Crythin Gifford?

Key quotation

Yet they had been, in some sense I did not understand, unreal ghostly, things that were dead.

(p. 82, l. 5)

Text focus

Read from the top of page 79 to the end of the paragraph at the top of page 81.

- Keckwick returns to collect Kipps at 2 a.m.
- The mist has cleared and Kipps realises that with the help of the brandy he must have slept for almost seven hours yet he does not feel refreshed.
- Make a note of what Keckwick does and says in this passage.
- What is strange about his body language and behaviour?
- Reconsider what you know about him so far and the role Susan Hill has created for him in the story.

Review your learning

(Answers given on pp. 86–87)

1. What does Kipps hear through the mist?
2. Why is Kipps shocked to see Keckwick at 2 a.m.?
3. Kipps now firmly believes that the woman in black is a ghost (p. 81). Explain how he came to this realisation.
4. Kipps is beginning to be haunted by the woman in black. What evidence can you find to support this idea in Chapter 6?

More interactive questions and answers online.

Grade *booster*

This chapter could be seen as the calm before the storm. Notice how the tension, built up in previous chapters, relaxed in the fifth chapter and is built up to a climax of terror at the end of this chapter, beginning with the rapid descending of the sea mist. Notice how often Hill builds and relaxes the tension. To attain the higher grades, you have to demonstrate 'thoughtful consideration' of the writer's style and the effect on the reader.

Chapter 7: Mr Jerome is Afraid

- Kipps decides to stay on in Crythin Gifford and complete his task.
- He goes to see Mr Jerome, Mrs Drablow's land agent, to ask for help in sorting out her papers and possessions.
- He learns that no-one will dare to help him.

Pause for thought

Consider why Mr Jerome being so perturbed adds to the mystery.

‖

Key quotation

He [Jerome] nodded. 'She saw no-one else. Not —' his voice trailed away.

'Not another living soul,' I [Kipps] put in evenly.

(p. 89, l. 13)

- Mr Jerome is visibly scared when Kipps tells him of the second apparition of the woman in black. He appears a broken man.
- Kipps now accepts that Eel Marsh House is haunted but in a fit of bravado determines to complete his business.

The next day, Kipps reassesses his situation and decides not to run back to London. He visits Mr Jerome to ask for help in sorting out Mrs Drablow's effects and learns that no-one but Keckwick will venture anywhere near Eel Marsh House. Mr Jerome is very afraid when Kipps tells him he saw the woman in black in the burial ground of the ruined monastery. The notion that she is a ghost becomes more acceptable to Kipps, although he makes light of it and becomes determined to carry out his task. Jerome appears to be a broken man.

Text focus

Re-read the whole of the passage which details Kipps' visit to the offices of Jerome, from page 87 to the middle of page 91.

- Think about what factual knowledge Kipps gains from this visit.
- Jerome informs Kipps that the only person Alice Drablow had contact with was Keckwick.
- Kipps' reply sounds rather clichéd. Normally 'not another living soul' is a glib phrase used with little thought behind it, yet here it suggests that Alice Drablow communed with souls which were not living, that is, ghosts. This Key quotation is a good one to use to demonstrate the use of irony in the text. Kipps is sounding sympathetic to Jerome by finishing his sentence for him, yet in reality he is pumping him for information. This is a very simple yet effective narrative technique which helps the reader to read between the lines and beyond.

Kipps returns to the Gifford Arms and writes a letter to Mr Bentley saying his task will take longer than he had anticipated. He borrows a bicycle and sets off exploring the countryside, hoping that the exercise will alleviate his mental anguish.

Grade *booster* **!**

A and A* candidates will be able to comment on the effective use of dialogue here. Susan Hill deliberately uses pause for effect so that when Kipps finishes Jerome's sentence, we as readers know that this is very significant.

Grade *booster* **!**

To attain the highest grades, be prepared to consider that the first-person narrative structure (see *Style*, p. 57) helps the reader identify more directly with Kipps' change of mood and emotions, in particular how the reader shares his feelings of fear and denial.

Review your learning

(Answers given on p. 87)

1 Why does Kipps change his mind about going back to London?

2 What new information does Kipps learn from his visit to Mr Horatio Jerome?

3 What is Kipps' state of mind in this chapter? Explain how he reacts to Mr Jerome's fear and panic.

More interactive questions and answers online.

Chapter 8: Spider

- Kipps decides to spend two nights at Eel Marsh House to complete his business.
- He goes to dinner at Mr Daily's house.
- Daily fails to dissuade him from staying at the house and lends him Spider, the dog for protection and companionship.

Feeling much better after his bike ride, Kipps returns to Crythin Gifford and meets Mr Daily, who invites him to dinner.

On returning to the inn, he informs the landlord that he wishes to retain his room but intends to spend a couple of nights at Eel Marsh House. Again he does not get any response.

Text focus

In the first two full paragraphs on page 96, Kipps informs the landlord of his intentions and the landlord says nothing at all.

- By this point in the story the conspiracy of silence is firmly established. 'Conspiracy of silence' is a term used to describe an agreement (spoken or unspoken) between a group of people, to say nothing and to give no information to others outside the group. Very often, they do not discuss the secret within the group either.
- Go back and look at the following references:
  - Daily's comments (p. 37).
  - The landlord's introduction (p. 42).
  - Mr Jerome (p. 47).
  - Kipps' conversation with a farmer (p. 56).
  - Keckwick's silence (p. 62).
  - Keckwick's behaviour (pp. 80–81).

Grade *booster*

When writing about structure, candidates aiming for the highest grades should show how the conspiracy of silence is built up by referring to the episodes above.

– Kipps' reflections on the landlord's behaviour (pp. 82–83).
– The landlord's willingness to discuss mundane matters but not Kipps' experience at Eel Marsh House (pp. 85–86).
– The whole of the encounter with Jerome, Chapter 7.
– Daily's warnings (in this chapter) to stay away from Eel Marsh House.

After an excellent dinner, Kipps learns more of Daily's financial success in the property market and begins to trust and admire his directness and honesty. He confides his plans to Daily who attempts to dissuade him from returning to Eel Marsh House. Kipps is adamant so Daily offers him his dog, Spider, for company.

Review your learning

(Answers given on p. 87)

1 How does Samuel Daily treat Kipps?
2 How is this different from the way the landlord treats him?
3 What do we learn about Daily's character from the way he speaks?

 More interactive questions and answers online.

Grade *booster*

Consider why Daily does not tell Kipps all he knows at this point in the story. AO1: respond to texts critically and imaginatively; select and evaluate relevant textual detail to illustrate and support interpretations. (See p. 71 for further explanation of AOs.)

Chapter 9: In the Nursery

● Kipps returns to Eel Marsh House with Spider.
● From Alice's letters he discovers that she adopted Nathaniel Pierston, the illegitimate son of a close relative.

- Again he hears the sound of the ghostly pony trap and the cries of the dying child.
- He discovers the source of the strange bumping sound and the nursery behind the locked door.

The next day, Kipps sets off on his bicycle to Eel Marsh House accompanied by Spider. After working all morning he ventures out in the burial ground but this time the visit is uneventful.

That night Kipps is woken by a strange bumping sound behind the locked door. The dog is alarmed.

The following morning the weather has changed. Kipps checks the locked door but cannot hear anything. He returns to the inn for more provisions. Back at the house he begins to read a bundle of letters written to Alice Drablow about 60 years earlier from someone called Jennet. He pieces together the following information.

- Jennet, a relative of Alice Drablow, was an unmarried mother who had been banished to Scotland and was being forced to give up her child for adoption.
- The letters formed a series of heart-breaking correspondence from which it is clear Jennet is desperate to keep her son.
- In the same packet there were adoption papers stating that Nathaniel Pierston, infant son of Jennet Humfrye, was to be adopted by Alice and Morgan Thomas Drablow.

Kipps is disturbed by the behaviour of the dog and hears the strange

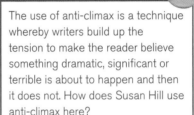

Pause for thought

The use of anti-climax is a technique whereby writers build up the tension to make the reader believe something dramatic, significant or terrible is about to happen and then it does not. How does Susan Hill use anti-climax here?

***Text* focus**

Social and historical context: page 120, line 12 to page 121, line 22.

- Study this description of a nineteenth-century nursery. What does it tell you about childhood at that time? Toys are believed to be educational and are used to help form children's values into adulthood. Consider the kind of toys which might be in a modern nursery. Clearly attitudes to gender, religion and race have changed over the last 150 years. What evidence can you find for this in this passage? Be prepared to comment on changes in attitudes and values. Remember to give a balanced and considered viewpoint.
- AO4: relate texts to their social, cultural and historical contexts and literary traditions. (See p. 72 for further explanation of AOs.)

bumping sound of the night before. He fetches an axe to break down the locked door and hears the sound of the ghostly pony trap and the terrible screams of the drowning child. The dog is paralysed with terror and Kipps has to carry her indoors.

Once inside, the dog is galvanised into action and returns to the locked door which is now open. Kipps realises the sound is that of a rocking chair on a wooden floor. On entering Kipps discovers a completely furnished child's nursery with all the clothes and toys beautifully preserved. He is overwhelmed by a great feeling of desolation and loss. Exhausted, he prepares for bed.

Grade *booster*

To access the higher grades you should be able to analyse how Susan Hill manipulates the reader's fears in this chapter, commenting particularly on the way tension is created and then relieved throughout the chapter.

Review your learning

(Answers given on p. 87)

1. How does Susan Hill use Spider the dog to build and relax tension in the story?
2. What is Kipps' bed-time reading and what does this show about his character?
3. Who was Rose Judd?

 More interactive questions and answers online.

Chapter 10: Whistle and I'll Come to You

- Kipps has another sleepless night due to the violent storm and the ghostly cries of a child.
- Spider nearly drowns.
- The woman in black appears at the nursery window.
- Kipps hears the sound of the pony trap again.

The title of this chapter is adapted from the title of another ghost story, *Oh Whistle and I'll Come to You, My Lad* written in 1910 by M. R. James.

That night Kipps lies awake listening to the violent storm. Again he hears the cries of the child. He gets up to make a drink and feels a ghostly presence.

He returns to his room for his torch, which he knocks off a table and breaks. Remembering there is a candle in the nursery, he fetches it.

In the morning Kipps takes Spider for a walk and hears a ghostly whistle. The dog bounds off and runs into quicksand. After a desperate struggle, Kipps manages to save her. He sees another vision of the woman in black watching them from the nursery window. The tension

Key quotation

I had simply the absolute certain sense of someone just having passed close to me and gone away down the corridor.

(p.124, l. 30)

mounts further when he hears the sound of a pony trap at the end of the causeway.

Text **focus**

Read page 126 from 'For a very long time,...' to the end of the first paragraph on page 127, '...enough to confront and overcome it'.

- This chapter illustrates Susan Hill's skill in developing and relaxing tension and suspense. The reader follows every twist and turn in Kipps' emotions and this is an example of first-person narrative at its finest.
- The first half of the chapter is the most terrifying. This is built entirely on the sounds of the storm, the darkness and the ghostly cries of a child. Affected by these elements, Kipps' imagination goes into overdrive to such an extent that he begins to doubt his own sanity.
- Examine the language in the passage. Make a list of words which evoke fear. Which are the most effective in scaring the reader?
- What does Kipps have to say about the effects of fear on the human psyche?

Review your learning

(Answers given on pp. 87–88)

① How would you describe Kipps' state of mind in Chapter 10?

② How do you think he has changed since he arrived in Crythin Gifford?

③ The large, isolated old house is a common feature in ghost stories. How does Hill use this to great effect in this chapter?

 More interactive questions and answers online.

Grade *booster*

Look carefully at the structure of the novel so far. The two main supernatural ingredients are the apparitions of the woman in black and the sounds of the pony and trap and the child sinking in the marshes. Note the different points in the story where these recur. AO2: explain how language, *structure* and form contribute to writers' presentation of ideas, themes and settings. (See p. 72 for further explanation of AOs.) Higher grade candidates will be able to recall clearly the points at which supernatural events occur and describe their cumulative effects on Kipps.

Chapter 11: A Packet of Letters

Pause for thought

What do you think of Samuel Daily?

- Kipps has collapsed and is revived by Samuel Daily who has arrived by pony and trap.
- Spider survives but is exhausted.
- Kipps visits the nursery for the last time.
- Kipps convalesces at Daily's home.
- Kipps reads Alice's papers and, with the help of Daily, pieces the mystery together.
- Stella arrives.

This time the sound of the pony and trap was real. Samuel Daily, unable to settle, arrives to find Kipps unconscious at the front of the house.

After carrying him indoors, he revives him and they pack up his belongings and Alice's papers. Kipps is deeply disturbed and hopes never to return to the house. He looks in on the nursery for the last time and finds it has been trashed. This compounds his terror.

Safely back at Daily's home, Kipps examines the papers and with the help of Daily discovers that Jennet Humfrye was the younger sister of Alice Drablow. She gave birth to Nathaniel Pierston and was forced to give up her illegitimate child for adoption to Alice and Thomas Drablow. Six years later the boy, his nursemaid, his dog and Keckwick's father took a wrong turning in the mist to Eel Marsh

> **Key quotation**
>
> **And wherever she has been seen… In some violent or dreadful circumstance, a child has died.**
>
> (p. 149, l. 27)

House and drowned in the marshes. Jennet Humfrye saw and heard it happen from the nursery window. Twelve years later she died of a wasting disease. Both the boy and his mother are buried in the graveyard of the old monastery beyond Eel Marsh House. The woman in black is the ghost of Jennet Humfrye and Kipps learns of her legacy.

All the villagers are terrified and Jerome especially, as he has lost a child.

Grade *booster*

Social/historical/cultural context: before the 1960s it was considered deeply shameful for unmarried women to give birth. Babies were often forcibly taken from them and offered for adoption. Candidates targeting the higher grades will recognise that this is a central point of the story and be able to discuss it in the context of the struggle between goodness and evil, for example can cruelty ever be justified in the name of righteousness?

Text focus

Read the end of page 150 from 'I asked myself unanswerable questions...' to the end of the first paragraph on page 151, '...a man might range himself on one side or the other'.

● Susan Hill is a Christian writer and *The Woman in Black* is a morality tale.

● 'Now, I realized that there were forces for good and those for evil doing battle together...' This idea is central to the Christian faith. Now you know the whole background to the woman in black, do you support the idea that Jennet is evil or a victim of evil? Does she deserve our sympathy or condemnation?

● How does Jennet's story fit your own ideas of Christianity?

These are some ideas for you to reflect on that will help you formulate an original, personal response. However Kipps' story is not yet complete. Your ideas and attitudes may change.

Kipps is deeply affected and develops a fever. In his sleep he is haunted by the woman in black and it takes him nearly two weeks to recover physically. His fiancée, Stella, comes to visit him.

Review your learning

(Answers given on p. 88)

❶ What is the connection between Keckwick and the woman in black?

❷ Why was Mr Jerome so afraid in Chapter 7?

❸ Now Kipps knows the full extent of what the villagers of Crythin Gifford have been keeping from him, how has it affected him?

 More interactive questions and answers online.

Grade *booster*

This is a long chapter that is followed by a short chapter. All the strands of the main story are brought together. The mystery is explained. Think about how Susan Hill has constructed the story (AO2, see p. 72) and how using the first-person narrative technique (see *Style*, p. 57) allows the main character to comment on events and reflect on his feelings at the time. To gain the highest grades, you need to comment on the advantages and disadvantages of using this technique.

Chapter 12: The Woman in Black

Pause for thought

Structure: Hill moves the story to the present. Kipps has come to the final part of his ghost story and has to steel himself to write it. Esmé has watched his distress while he has 'relived those past horrors', now he has to finish what he started. Why do you think the writer uses this technique? What do you think it adds to the narrative?

- Stella and Kipps return to London and marry six weeks later.
- At Kipps' request, Mr Bentley does not involve him further in Alice Drablow's affairs.
- A year later Stella gives birth to a son.
- A year after that, the woman in black reappears and causes the deaths of Stella and the boy.
- Kipps concludes his story.

The next day Stella takes Kipps back to London. He resolves to stay in touch with Daily and books a puppy when they decide to breed from Spider. He does not return to the town again.

Six weeks after their return, Stella and Kipps marry. Mr Bentley gives Kipps more responsibility and a pay-rise though Eel Marsh House is not mentioned again.

A year later Stella gives birth to a son and Samuel Daily becomes his godfather. The small family settles into domestic bliss until the following summer when they visit a large London park. The child is too frightened to ride a donkey alone so Stella takes him for a ride around the park in a pony and trap. Kipps is an onlooker as the woman in black appears from behind a tree. She startles the pony, which bolts, throwing the child to his death against a tree. Stella suffers broken legs and a broken neck and dies ten months later.

The story ends abruptly. The ghost of Jennet Humfrye has had her revenge.

Text focus

A central belief of Christianity is that all sins are forgivable. Now the story is complete do you believe that Jennet Humfrye cannot be forgiven?

- Re-read page 158, line 20, to the end of the first paragraph on page 159 '…the woman had disappeared'. The woman in black appears for the final time and completes her mission.
- What are your feelings about Jennet Humfrye now? Can evil ever ultimately triumph over good?
- The story completes its full circle and ends where it began, back at Monk's Piece, Arthur Kipps having completed his manuscript. It ends on a bitter note.
- The story has reached its climax. The *Daily Express* has described it as 'Heartstoppingly chilling'. The *Guardian* described it as, 'A rattling good yarn, the sort that chills the mind as well as the spine.'
- There is a brief reference to Esmé's family. 'They' asked for his story and now he has told it. The novel ends with a one word sentence: 'Enough'.

Key quotation

They [the stepchildren] asked for my story. I have told it. Enough.

(p. 160, l. 5)

Review your learning

(Answers given on p. 88)

1 Ghost stories are at their most effective when shared and read aloud. How would you read the last word? Give reasons for your opinion.

2 Jot down your feelings now you have come to the end of the novel.

More interactive questions and answers online.

Grade *booster*

The story ends abruptly with three short sentences. Why is it so abrupt? Do you think the ending is effective? Remember there are no right answers to questions on effectiveness as you are invited to share your thoughts as an individual with the examiner and to show your appreciation of the writer's craft. However, you must always refer to the reader and to the writer's purpose in your examination answer. Marks in the highest grade bands will be awarded to students who show insight and originality of response.

Timeline

The actual time in which the novel is set is vague. Susan Hill says the main storyline (where Kipps spends time in Crythin Gifford) is set between 1900 and 1914. From this it is possible to work out approximate times for other events in the novel. It is important to understand the timeline of the novel in order to understand its structure (AO2, see p. 72).

Chapter	What happens	Timing
1: Christmas Eve	Arthur Kipps, a man in his fifties, feels compelled to write his own, personal and true ghost story, spurred on by refusing his step-children's request to contribute to the frivolous Christmas Eve ghost-story-telling session	Christmas Eve sometime in the 1930s
2: A London Particular	The 21-year-old Arthur Kipps, a junior solicitor, is sent to Crythin Gifford by his employer, Mr Bentley, to attend the funeral of Alice Drablow and to sort out her effects	Sometime between 1900 and 1914
3: The Journey North	He travels by train from London, King's Cross via Crewe to Homerby	Monday
4: The Funeral of Mrs Drablow	Kipps encounters the woman in black for the first time at Alice Drablow's funeral	Tuesday
5: Across the Causeway	Kipps visits Eel Marsh House	Tuesday afternoon

Chapter	What happens	Timing
6: The Sound of a Pony and Trap	Kipps hears the sound of a pony and trap sinking in the marshes and the cries of a dying child	Tuesday evening
	Keckwick returns to collect Kipps	2 a.m. Wednesday morning
7: Mr Jerome is Afraid	Kipps visits Mr Jerome	Wednesday
8: Spider	Kipps goes to Samuel Daily's for dinner	Wednesday evening
9: In the Nursery	Kipps returns to Eel Marsh House alone except for the dog	Thursday
10: Whistle and I'll Come to You	Kipps feels the ghostly presence. He nearly drowns in his successful attempt to save Spider	Thursday and the early hours of Friday morning
11: A Packet of Letters	Rescued by Samuel Daily. They return to Crythin Gifford and examine Alice Drablow's papers	Friday
	All the details of the story are revealed	Flashback to sometime in the 1850s
	Kipps collapses and is ill for approximately 12 days	Friday
	Kipps returns to London	Twelve days later
	He marries his fiancée, Stella	Six weeks later
12: The Woman in Black	Tragedy strikes. Arthur Kipps is then a widower for a further 13 years until he marries Esmé, a widow with four children	A year later, sometime between 1900 and 1914
	14 years later, the family gathers at Monk's Piece for Christmas	Christmas Eve sometime in the 1930s
	The story comes full circle. Kipps has written his story	In the New Year sometime in the 1930s

Review your learning

(Answers given on p. 88)

Photocopy the timeline and enter the exact page references for each chapter and each event. This will help you to familiarise yourself with the layout and help you navigate through the text more quickly. Please note that no answer is given for this task because it is the process of finding out that is important, not the actual answers.

More interactive questions and answers online.

Structure

Whereas the **plot** of the novel is the sequence of events, that is what happens, the **structure** of the book involves the shape that these events take or the pattern they form.

The structure of the ghost story is relatively simple and can easily be understood from the timeline. The story is clearly not **chronological** (i.e. the events are not presented in date and time order). For instance, Chapter 1 is set approximately 30 years after the main story. The main character, Arthur Kipps, is telling of his experience with the woman in black. The writer is using the first-person narrative technique (see *Style*, p. 57). In the final lines of the book, Kipps, the narrator, returns to the present, having told his story.

This is the basic structure of the novel, though there are occasions where the writer interrupts the sequence of events to comment on the action, for instance page 44, line 9.

Here Susan Hill uses the older, experienced Arthur Kipps to comment on his younger self in order to establish his character and to voice her views. This is a technique used frequently by Charles Dickens in *A Christmas Carol* but he uses it to poke fun at the government of the time whereas Hill uses it to create a sense of foreboding.

The main story begins in Chapter 2, 'A London Particular', in Mr Bentley's London chambers. This establishes the context. Arthur Kipps is sent to Crythin Gifford to wind up the affairs of the deceased Alice Drablow. During the period of one week he is haunted to such an extent that he suffers from nervous exhaustion and is confined to his sick room at Samuel Daily's house for a further 12 days, after which he returns to London believing his ordeal to be over. However, nearly two years after his return, the ghost reappears and exacts the most devastating retribution on him for interfering in the affairs of Alice Drablow.

> **Key quotation**
>
> For I see that then I was still all in a state of innocence, but that innocence, once lost, is lost for ever.
>
> (p. 44, l. 9)

The structure of the novel can be seen as being almost circular as it ends, back where it began, at Monk's Piece. It began on Christmas Eve. Arthur Kipps decided to write about his ghostly encounter and the story is completed in the following New Year. Although this is the outline of the main structure, it is an oversimplification as at various points of the narrative, particularly the most terrifying times, the older Kipps makes sense of his feelings using hindsight. An example of this appears on pages 150 and 151 where he interrupts his account of events and attempts to make sense of his dreams in terms of his religious upbringing.

Key quotation

Then perhaps I should finally be free of it for whatever life remained for me to enjoy.

(p. 22, l. 24)

It is a useful exercise to go back and read Chapter 1 immediately after you have completed the final chapter. Although the opening doesn't carry on exactly where the final chapter ceases, it does fill in some of the gaps between those dreadful days and the present. It answers some of the questions concerning what happens to Kipps. Clearly Mr Bentley took him under his wing and eventually nurtured him back to a state of normality where he began to cope with life. The point of Kipps writing his narrative is to escape his terrors once and for all.

Review your learning

(Answers given on p. 88)

Using the information from the text, describe Kipps' life in the years between losing Stella and the Christmas Eve of Chapter 1. The evidence doesn't necessarily have to be factual but it needs to fit what you already know about character, action and plot.

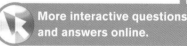

More interactive questions and answers online.

Characterisation

- Who's who in *A Woman in Black*?
- What is the difference between character and characterisation?
- Which characters are rounded and developed and which are not?
- How does Hill reveal the characters to us?
- What evidence can we find to help us assess each character?

Who's who in *A Woman in Black*?

- Arthur Kipps — a middle-aged lawyer, the narrator of the story
- Esmé — Kipps' second wife
- Isobel, Oliver, Will and Edmund — Esmé's children from her marriage to Captain Ainley
- Aubrey Pearce — Isobel's husband, father of her three young sons
- Mr Bentley — a renowned solicitor, Kipps' employer and later his business partner
- Tomes — Mr Bentley's clerk
- Mrs Alice Drablow — Mr Bentley's dead client
- Mr Samuel Daily — a prosperous land dealer in Crythin Gifford who becomes Arthur's friend and protector
- Mrs Daily — his wife
- Stella — Arthur Kipps fiancée and first wife
- Mr Jerome — Alice Drablow's land agent
- The landlord of the Gifford Arms — landlord of the inn where Arthur Kipps stays
- Jennet Humfrye — the woman in black, Alice Drablow's sister
- Nathaniel Pierston — Jennet Humfrye's illegitimate son who is adopted by her sister, Alice Drablow
- Keckwick — Mrs Drablow's man Friday, who drives the pony and trap as his father did before him
- Spider — Daily's dog, lent to Kipps to be his companion at Eel Marsh House
- Rose Judd — Nathaniel Pierston's nurse, killed with him and Keckwick's father in the tragic accident on the marshes

Grade *booster*

Remember, to gain marks in the higher grades (A*–C) you must write about characterisation, not just about characters but their role in the story. The difference is that you show awareness of the fact that the characters are not real people but have been constructed by the author to fulfil her purpose — in this case to tell a good ghost story and to frighten the reader. The genre is much more important than character and for this reason some of the characters are hardly developed beyond being functional.

Arthur Kipps

Arthur Kipps is both the main character and the narrator. In order to enjoy the story, the reader must be sympathetic to him and share his feelings. For a ghost story to be successful the reader must share his fear vicariously. Hill makes this very easy for the reader through the use of first-person narrative: Kipps tells his own story.

In the first and last chapters we see him as a man approaching old age, a retired lawyer who has settled into the safety of Monk's Piece with his wife and family ready to enjoy Christmas. One of the first things we learn about him is how his 'spirits have for many years now been excessively affected by the ways of the weather'. Nevertheless, he enjoys country pursuits such as walking and shooting with dogs. He smokes a pipe and looks forward to a peaceful Christmas with his family, that is until he renews his 'close acquaintance…with mortal dread and terror of spirit' (p. 15, l. 17).

Dan Kremer as Arthur Kipps in the Utah Shakespearean Festival's 2009 production of *The Woman in Black* (photo by Karl Hugh)

Kipps is clearly shaken by his step-sons' harmless pursuit of telling ghost stories at Christmas and resolves to exorcise his own ghost by writing his story in the New Year. Until then he feels protected by his strong Christian beliefs.

In the final chapter Kipps is completely exhausted. With great difficulty, he overcomes the paralysis that prevents him from completing his story. He alarms his wife by his strange behaviour, his wanderings in all weathers, his silence and his distress. He eventually 'uses the very last of [his] strength' to finish his story and almost collapses when it is told. His final word is an exhausted 'Enough'. His intention is that the world will only know of his 'past horrors' when his wife reads his manuscript after his death.

Before he begins his tale, Arthur Kipps appears to be a very different character from his youthful self. Once he begins to tell his story, the

Utah Shakespearean Festival

reader can recognise the courage, the strength and the ambition of youth. The young Arthur Kipps is unremarkable. His life is typical of a young man of his social class and the period in which he lived. He is privileged, well educated, ambitious, adventurous, impatient, arrogant, brave and foolhardy. He is eager for responsibility and anxious to be promoted within his firm of lawyers.

In Chapter 2, Kipps describes his young self as 'a sturdy, common-sensical young fellow' (p. 26, l.8) with 'a blithe spirit' and 'a schoolboy's passion for everything to do with railway stations and journeys on steam locomotives'. He makes a rash judgement about Samuel Daily 'in my youthful and priggish way, summed up and all but dismissed him' (p. 36, l. 33) yet is very proud to announce to Daily that he is Alice Drablow's solicitor. Once settled into the Gifford Arms, he begins to feel like a man on holiday although he is both 'curious and a little irritated by his [the landlord's] manner' (p. 42, l. 22). He had the youthful arrogance to assume that he was superior to the people of Crythin Gifford.

> ### Key quotation
>
> **For I must confess I had the Londoner's sense of superiority in those days.**
>
> (p. 42, l. 30)

Throughout his tale, Arthur Kipps keeps returning to the present to remind the reader of the change in himself. When he began his quest he was 'still in a state of innocence' (p. 44, l. 10) but his warning that 'innocence, once lost, is lost forever' fills the reader with dread.

Like any intelligent young man, Kipps is observant and studies people carefully. He is aware he is not being told the full truth in answer to his questions. Yet he is kind-hearted and sensitive enough to feel the sadness in the fact that no friend or relative was present at Alice Drablow's funeral and is heartened when he sees the woman in black for the first time, mistaking her for a genuine mourner.

When Kipps is first introduced to Eel Marsh House his romantic nature is evident. He is stunned by the beauty of its surroundings and he imagines himself and his fiancée Stella living there. He continues to explore, marvelling at the wonder of nature and imagining the place during different seasons of the year. However, his feelings change suddenly when he sees the woman in black again in the graveyard.

> ### Key quotation
>
> **...at that moment I was far from able to base my reactions upon reason and logic.**
>
> (p. 65, l. 27)

He is filled with fear, his flesh creeps and his knees tremble (p. 65). He is 'gripped and held fast by such dread and horror and apprehension of evil'. This is a turning point in his life. Never before has he experienced such fear, though he still retains sufficient youthful curiosity to be 'consumed with the desire to find out exactly who it was that I had seen' (p. 67, l. 19).

At this point he states 'I did not believe in ghosts'. He goes on to qualify his statement 'Or rather, until this day, I had not done so'. He believed himself to be a rational and sensitive young man who based his beliefs on evidence. He is deeply frightened by his experience and his fear is compounded further when the sea mists (or frets) descend and he hears the 'appalling last noises of a pony and trap, carrying a child in it… being dragged under by the quicksand and the pull of the incoming tide' (p. 75, l. 1).

Even later, when fortified by brandy, he longs for the safety of London and the comfort of being with Stella and friends. His feelings turn to anger and he eventually exhausts himself, wallows in self-pity, drinks a second glass of brandy and sinks into oblivion. His reactions to adversity are those of a typical young man and he suffers the extreme emotions of fear and resorts to alcohol for respite. Even when rescued by Keckwick in the dead of night from Eel Marsh House, he resolves to return to London and leave Alice Drablow's business in the hands of Mr Jerome.

However, in the cold light of day, his courage returns and he is determined to see his last task through to the end, although this time he is 'deliberately making myself sound carefree and cheerful' (p. 91, l. 12). After a rejuvenating bicycle ride he admits to feeling 'like a new man, proud, satisfied…' (p. 94, l. 10). He is defiant and cheerful and, ignoring Samuel Daily's advice, returns to Eel Marsh House with Spider for comfort and protection.

Kipps' character is wholly believable and fully rounded. He is completely human and reacts to others in a normal way. Hill introduces some humour, for instance Kipps does not let Samuel Daily know he arrived at his house by bicycle as it is not a sufficiently sophisticated mode of transport to fit the image he wishes to create. It is these small details that help the reader to identify closely with the main character and share his terrifying experiences.

After the death of Stella and the baby Kipps is a broken man. He gradually recovers and he lives for his work and collects watercolours. The middle-aged Kipps bears no resemblance to his youthful self. He tells of how his recovery only began 12 years after the tragedy when he discovered Monk's Piece and resolved to buy it. It is several years later when it comes on the market and he marries Esmé Ainley that it becomes his family home.

Mr Bentley

Mr Bentley is a Victorian gentleman who has chambers in London and speaks in an old-fashioned way. 'Sit ye down' and 'Don't you know' are two of his favourite expressions. He calls some of his clients 'rum 'uns', including Alice Drablow. He likes to tell a good story and Kipps is unsure when he is embellishing the facts. He suffers from gout, disease that was thought at the time to be caused by rich food and excessive alcohol consumption, although this was later disproved by the medical profession.

Mr Bentley is a moderate and kind man. He is head of the family firm of solicitors and has many important clients for example Lord Boltrope. Initially Arthur Kipps' employer, he later accepts Kipps as partner in his firm of solicitors. He acts as a father figure to Kipps and looks after him following his ordeal as he blames himself for what happens. He treats Kipps like someone convalescing after an illness or accident. He is anxious to see Kipps settled in a house of his own and encourages him to buy Monk's Piece.

Everything we know about Bentley is from the first two chapters.

When he retires he becomes a county magistrate, churchwarden, governor of many parish boards, bodies and committees. He takes his public duties very seriously and dies at the age of 81.

Tomes

Tomes is Mr Bentley's clerk and Susan Hill gives him a name meaning large books. He is of little significance to the plot but adds style, light relief and gentle humour to the story. He is a thin little man who is confined to a cubby hole where he receives visitors and keeps ledgers. He has a permanent cold and sniffs constantly. He reminds clients of their own mortality, which is very apt as their business is usually connected to making a last will and testament.

Samuel Daily

Samuel Daily is in his late fifties when Kipps meets him on the train to Homerby. He is a big man with a beefy face and huge, raw-looking hands. He is well spoken, although he has a local accent. He looks like a prosperous farmer or small-business owner. He is a self-made man and has acquired his wealth by buying and selling land. He is a family man who appears to be embarrassed by his wealth but continues to build his business for the benefit of his son and grandson. He is unpopular with the local people because of his success but even his rivals in business believe that Daily would not attempt to profit by buying up any of Alice Drablow's estate. He represents the *nouveau riche*: he is friendly and hospitable, but he speaks in a guarded manner especially on the subject of Alice Drablow.

Grade *booster*

Samuel Daily is made to seem like a guardian angel to Kipps. He supports and advises him but doesn't tell him what to do as this would alienate him. He is inquisitive, friendly and plainspoken. Like his name, he represents normality. He and the landlord are described by Kipps as 'sturdy men of good commonsense'. Daily is a shrewd judge of character and when he accuses Kipps of 'whistling in the dark' — a metaphor for convincing himself that he is not afraid and bewildered — Kipps acknowledges the truth of the statement (p. 95).

When invited to Daily's house for dinner, Kipps admires his simplicity and directness, recognises his astuteness and honesty (p. 98) and begins to warm to him and confide in him. However, when Daily states bluntly 'You're a fool if you go on with it' (p. 98, l. 12), Kipps comes up with several reasons why he feels compelled to reveal the secrets of Eel Marsh House. Seeing his determination, Daily offers him Spider for protection, comfort and companionship.

Pause for thought

Do you think Kipps and Daily would have maintained contact after the deaths of Stella and the baby? Make sure you can back up your view with evidence related to the text.

Although a down-to-earth, practical man, Daily acts upon his instincts and, fortunately for Kipps, he feels compelled to come to his aid at Eel Marsh House. Daily is not too proud to accept that supernatural forces are at work. Their friendship is consolidated and Kipps returns to stay at Daily's house to continue his work on Alice Drablow's papers, and to recover from his near-death experiences and his terrifying encounters with the woman in black. Having discovered the history of Jennet Humfrye from the papers, Kipps is ready to listen to what Daily knows and learns the reason for the villagers' fear.

Daily and his wife look after Kipps during his illness and they remain firm friends when Kipps returns to London. Although Kipps never returns to Crythin Gifford, Daily visits him and Stella in London and he becomes their baby son's godfather and the baby is given the name Samuel as one of his Christian names. This is the last we hear of Samuel Daily as his role in the story is complete.

Mrs Daily

Pause for thought

How do you think a woman of Mrs Daily's social status would spend her time?

Mrs Daily waits on her husband and his guest and tends to Kipps during his illness, but like the other wives and girlfriends in the story, does not play a major role and is not a developed character in the story.

> ### Key quotation
>
> 'Mrs Daily was a quiet shy-seeming, powdery-looking little woman...' who '... said little, smiled nervously, crocheted something elaborate with very fine cotton.'
>
> (p. 97, l. 14)

Keckwick

Kipps is led by Jerome to expect that Keckwick will be very obliging. When they first meet there appears to be little to distinguish him from his pony and his most startling characteristic is his silence. It is only when he returns to pick up Kipps from Eel Marsh House that he speaks. He is very blunt and matter of fact when commenting on the weather, although he refuses to be drawn on the ghostly sounds. Kipps appreciates Keckwick's generosity in putting himself out for a stranger and caring enough to venture out in the middle of the night to fetch him. Keckwick's kindness to Alice Drablow was also remarkable as he was the only 'living soul' (as opposed to the soul of her dead sister) with whom she had contact, although strangely he did not attend her funeral. The reader may feel that some amnesty was reached between him and the ghost: he also suffered a great loss when the child drowned as his father was driving the pony and trap and died also.

Keckwick is presented as being physically very unattractive '...his nose and much of the lower part of his face were covered in bumps and lumps and warts and...the skin was porridgy in texture and a dark livid red' (p. 79, l. 32). No explanation is given for this, but it does help to create a very visual and disturbing picture, a totally appropriate image for a ghost story.

Pause for thought

Why do you think that Keckwick did not attend Alice Drablow's funeral? Remember to support your views with textual reference.

The landlord

Kipps gleaned from the layout of the town that the inhabitants were very inward-looking and huddled together for protection against the elements. This is a metaphor for the conspiracy of silence. Nobody will talk about the woman in black, especially not to a stranger. The landlord of the Gifford Arms is not named. His role is to provide an air of mystery around the Drablow affairs and to frustrate Kipps with his enigmatic comments.

He is at the centre of the conspiracy of silence and his purpose in the story is to provide Kipps and the reader with background information and to add to the tension and suspense. The landlord is more significant for what he does not say rather than for what he does say.

As with all the characters, we see the landlord only through the eyes of the young Kipps but it is possible to read beyond Kipps' youthful impatience. Clearly the landlord runs a thriving business. He is at the centre of the activities on market day and it is in his commercial interest not to exploit what he knows of the circumstances surrounding the woman in black. Nevertheless, like Samuel Daily and Keckwick, he is concerned about Kipps' welfare and is there to welcome him back from Eel Marsh House in the middle of the night.

Pause for thought

Do you consider the character of the landlord to be sufficiently developed to be believable? Support your ideas with reference to the text.

The woman in black

When he first sees the woman in black Kipps mistakes her for a devoted friend of Alice Drablow. In fact the woman in black is the ghost of Jennet Humfrye, although this information is withheld from Kipps and the reader until it is confirmed by Samuel Daily in the penultimate chapter.

Key quotation

...it seemed poignant that a woman, who was perhaps only a short time away from her own death, should drag herself to the funeral of another.

(p. 49, l. 16)

Approximately 60 years before Alice Drablow's death, her 18-year-old, unmarried sister, Jennet Humfrye gave birth to a baby boy who was taken from her against her will and adopted by Alice and her husband. The child, Nathaniel Pierston, drowned at the age of six, together with Rose Judd, his nurse, and Keckwick senior when the pony and trap carrying them across the marshes lost its way in the mist and sank into the quicksand. After suffering from a dreadful wasting disease, Jennet Humfrye died 12 years later of heart failure. Kipps finds this information among Alice Drablow's papers. What he learns from Daily is not talked about in the village, namely that ever since her death, the ghost of Jennet has been seeking revenge on her sister at Eel Marsh House, and sightings of her have occurred out on the marshes, in the burial grounds and the surrounding areas. Every time the ghost is seen, a child dies in violent and dreadful circumstances. As a result, the villagers live in constant fear and dread.

It is only on his second encounter with the woman in black that it occurs to Kipps that she is a malevolent spirit.

Pause for thought

Look at the work you did for Text focus in *Plot and structure* on Chapter 4. How does Kipps' attitude to the ghost change from her first appearance on page 48?

Text focus

Re-read the text from the last paragraph on page 64 up to the end of the first four lines on page 66.

● Pick out the clues the writer gives to suggest that the woman in black is a supernatural presence.
● Make a note of the 'ingredients' that create the atmosphere surrounding her appearance. Look particularly at the light, the sounds, the plants and birds in the small burial ground.
● Make notes on the woman's physical appearance. Pick out words which are connected with evil.
● What do you think is the significance of the words in italics?

Katie Wackowski in the
Utah Shakespearean
Festival's 2009 production
of *The Woman in Black*
(photo by Karl Hugh)

Utah Shakespearean Festival

Kipps' first two encounters with the woman in black are visual but she doesn't confine her presence to apparitions. Her hauntings are manifested in the dreadful sounds of a child drowning, the mysterious sound of the creaking rocking chair, the nursery door that is locked and unlocked despite having no bolts or locks and her presence in Arthur Kipps' dreams.

By the time Spider is lured by a ghostly whistle into the quicksand, neither the reader nor Kipps doubts the ghost's evil intentions.

By the final chapter, all the mystery appears to be solved. Alice Drablow has been buried. Eel Marsh House has been abandoned and the woman in black has not re-appeared. Moreover, no child has died.

Kipps prays that 'the chain is broken — that her power is at an end — that she has gone — and I was the last ever to see her' (p. 155, l. 15). Nevertheless the reader knows the story cannot end here. The ghost will have her revenge and it will take the most horrendous form. As soon as the pony and trap is seen in the London park, it is evident whose child will die.

Mr Jerome

Mr Horatio Jerome was Alice Drablow's land agent and Kipps first meets him on the morning of her funeral. He is a strange little man who wears a 'shuttered expression' which reveals nothing of his personality. Kipps does not find out until much later that he is one of the woman in black's victims, having lost a child in tragic circumstances. Mr Jerome's appearance is very distinctive. He has a domed head fringed with gingerish hair which resembles a lampshade. His large eyes protrude and are the colour of gulls' eggs. In different circumstances he would probably look quite comical but his obvious fear and panic when Kipps mentions the young woman is startling to the reader and clearly frightens Kipps. Nevertheless, the moment passes, but the situation is not resolved.

The second time they meet is in Jerome's office. Kipps has gone there to seek help with his task but Jerome clearly refuses to become involved other than to say the only person who may help is Keckwick. Ironically, it is Jerome's evident terror, '…his hands…were working, rubbing, fidgeting, gripping and ungripping in agitation' (p. 88, l. 14) which forces Kipps to accept that he must solve the mystery of the woman in black. They both share the knowledge that they have been haunted, '…it took us to the very edge of the horizon where life and death meet together' (p. 90, l. 22) and it is not until Daily informs Kipps in the penultimate chapter that Jerome lost a child that Kipps realises what it was that had 'broken' him.

Alice Drablow

Alice Drablow was an old eccentric client of Mr Bentley's father. Kipps is sent to represent the firm at her funeral and to begin to sort out her legal affairs. She died alone at the age of 87 and had no living relatives except a great-niece and great-nephew who have lived in India for 40 years and are due to inherit her estate. Her funeral is attended only by undertaker's men, Kipps and Mr Jerome, people she did business with. She appears to have had no friends.

From the outset, mystery seems to surround her. Mr Bentley has to consider carefully whether or not she had children, Mr Daily's enigmatic comments make Kipps shudder, the landlord's reaction to her name is one of alarm. Mr Jerome, her land agent, is no more forthcoming except to say that Keckwick acted as go-between with the world beyond Eel Marsh House. Jerome says she saw no-one else. So, Kipps is left to build up his own profile of the reclusive old woman.

Kipps is surprised by the normality of the inside of Eel Marsh House and when he settles to read her papers he begins to piece together her life. The facts appear to be that she was married to Morgan Thomas Drablow and did not have any children except an adopted boy, Nathaniel Pierston, who was the biological son of her sister, Jennet Humfrye. Near the end of the story Kipps realises that the woman in black has been haunting Alice Drablow in Eel Marsh House for over half a century, taking her revenge to the extent that Alice Drablow's sanity was questionable. Nothing else was known of Alice Drablow and it is left to the reader to imagine what horrors she experienced.

> ### *Text* **focus**
>
> Read from the middle of page 146, line 16, to the middle of page 148.
> - Write down your impressions of Alice Drablow and the life she led. Remember to take into account the social climate of the time when making judgements about her character. Also take into account what the other characters have said about her and the way people behaved towards her when she was alive.

Stella

Stella is not a fully developed character because she is part of the normal world which Kipps left behind when he embarked on his adventure. She is on the periphery of the story until the final chapter, although Kipps frequently returns to his memories of her for comfort throughout his ordeal. We learn little of her character other than that she is the ideal support for a man of that time. She is always quietly in the background, a dutiful fiancée and later wife, who rescues him from Crythin Gifford and bears him a child (Joseph Arthur Samuel). Note that Samuel Daily's wife and Esmé, Kipps' second wife play very similar roles and are equally undeveloped. Their role in the novel is to support their husbands. Any further embellishment of their characters would distract the reader from the strictly controlled development of the ghost story.

Esmé and her family

The Ainley family provides a domestic context and a background of normality from which Kipps can tell his ghost story. The reader is introduced to them in Chapter 1 but they play no part in the rest of the story. Originally, Susan Hill intended to include a preface using the voice of a grown-up Oliver Ainley to explain the effect of the discovery of Kipps' manuscript on the rest of the family, but this was discarded. Clearly she decided it was more effective for Kipps' terrible experience to speak for itself.

Pause for thought

What does the characterisation of the women in the novel suggest to you about attitudes to women at the time Kipps is writing his manuscript? Be aware that this can be related to the social and historical context of the time.

Review your learning

(Answers given on pp. 88–89)

1. In your view, which character in *The Woman in Black* is most successfully presented?
2. How does Susan Hill make Kipps interesting?
3. Why do you think Mr Bentley blames himself for what happens to Kipps?
4. Why was Kipps pleased to see the woman in black at the funeral?
5. What does Kipps' reluctance to let Samuel Daily know he travelled to his house for dinner by bicycle show about his character?
6. With which character in the story do you have most sympathy? Give reasons for your answer.

More interactive questions and answers online.

Themes

- What are the novel's main themes?
- What do they add to the novel?
- How do themes work?
- What do you learn about Susan Hill's views from the themes she explores in *The Woman in Black*?

Although a ghost story is written primarily to entertain the reader, there is a serious message behind *The Woman in Black*. Susan Hill says, 'This is a story about evil; about how suffering and grief can warp a human personality'.

A theme is a concept or an idea that is explored in a novel. It runs like a thread throughout the story and can be looked at and examined in relation to other themes that are being explored.

There are usually several themes in a novel and many of them overlap. For instance, Susan Hill describes herself as a Christian writer. This is different from being a writer who happens to be Christian. She has also said that the only thing worth writing about is the inner self. One interpretation of this could be a reference to the spiritual nature of human beings and how their behaviour and sense of moral responsibility are affected by what happens to them. It could be for these reasons that the following themes are explored in some detail.

Revenge

The point about *The Woman in Black* is that revenge can never be good, can never succeed ultimately, and will never pay. 'Vengeance is mine, saith the Lord. I will repay.' (Romans 12:19)

Justice is one thing, revenge is very different. I also believe that after experiencing great distress or grief, a terrible life-experience, a person must eventually — though it may take a long time — leave it to rest and move on. The ghost in *The Woman in Black* goes on and on wreaking revenge on the innocent for what has happened to her, even after death. She has never let go, can never move on. As she could not in life, so she cannot after life.

These are Susan Hill's own views based on her Christian faith. The idea that it is wrong to seek revenge is central to Christianity. On page 155 Kipps describes the woman in black as having been 'a poor, crazed, troubled woman, dead of grief and distress, filled with hatred and desire for revenge'. At this point in the story where he is about to leave Daily's house to return to London with Stella, Kipps is almost sympathetic towards the ghost of Jennet Humfrye. He goes on to say that her actions are understandable but not forgivable. This is interesting as Kipps purports to be a Christian yet the Church teaches that God is mercy and, providing a sinner repents, all sins are forgivable.

Justice

Justice is related to vengeance. Ideas of justice are intertwined with notions of revenge. The Christian faith recognises that injustice is endemic in all societies and, although people strive for justice, it is not attainable as human beings' definition of justice is affected by the social norms of the time. Christians believe that God will provide justice (hopefully tempered with mercy) on judgement day. The reader is left with the larger questions to ponder — what happens to the spirit of Jennet Humfrye? Is she condemned to wander the earth for eternity? Can evil ultimately triumph? All good literature makes us think about the human condition. This is essentially a Christian story and it might be argued that it can teach us something about the way human beings should be treated and how they can triumph over disaster.

> **Grade *booster***
>
> The concept of justice is a difficult one. Again, A and A* candidates will be able to discuss this concept and offer textual reference in support of their views.

Religious faith

Kipps' story can be seen as a journey from innocence to experience, similar to the descriptions Christians often give of their lives as a journey through faith. His own religious background only begins to be meaningful to him once he is tested. 'I asked myself unanswerable questions about life and death and the borderlands between and I prayed, direct and simple, passionate prayers.' (p. 150, l. 29)

Before he encountered the woman in black his attitude towards religion was 'formal and dutiful'. Afterwards he realises that he believes there is a constant battle between the forces of good and evil and that every person must actively choose the side of goodness.

Fear

See *Sample essays* (pp. 76–79). The theme of fear is explored in detail in this section.

Katie Wackowski and James Stellos in the Utah Shakespearean Festival's 2009 production of *The Woman in Black* (photo by Karl Hugh)

Utah Shakespearean Festival

Nature and the supernatural

Susan Hill relies on the natural world: country and city landscapes; the rhythm and change of the seasons; and particularly the weather to establish an atmosphere of normality — a natural sequence of events, a natural backdrop to the story. For human beings life is experienced through the five senses: sight, hearing, touch, taste and smell. Once a **sixth sense** (which manifests itself as an awareness that doesn't come through any of the five senses) becomes apparent, the story moves into the realm of the supernatural. It is important for the reader to establish a definition of what is natural. Usually our understanding of nature is based on scientific reality. 'Supernatural' literally means beyond the natural, so supernatural events cannot be explained by reason or scientific theory.

In the first chapter, Arthur Kipps first refers to what he later calls a sixth sense — a knowledge, indeed a certainty, that Monk's Piece was one day to be his home (p. 13). He writes as if this was somehow preordained. This does in fact become reality years later although it could simply have

> **Key quotation**
>
> **I had no sense of having been here before, but an absolute conviction that I would come here again, that the house was already mine, bound to me invisibly.**
>
> (p. 12, l. 27)

been that he saw the house, liked it and bought it when it came on the market. Nevertheless, he definitely believes that he was led to the house by forces beyond nature. It is almost as if he has found his spiritual home.

In the main story, the sense of the supernatural tentatively begins with the first appearance of the woman in black, but on the second sighting this same feeling of certainty overtakes Kipps to such an extent that his life-long scepticism concerning ghosts is replaced by conviction. This is a crucial turning point in the novel. It is Kipps' first close encounter with evil.

Text **focus**

Study page 81, line 4 to page 82, line 5.
- Finally Kipps admits that he believes the woman in black to be a ghost and furthermore that the sound of the pony and trap sinking had been 'ghostly also'.
- From this passage, make a note of the words that suggest a world beyond reality, for instance 'eerily', 'unimagined', 'dreamed', 'not…real', 'not substantial'. How many more can you identify?
- Note the length of this paragraph and the amount of detail used by Kipps to describe what was happening to him. How do you feel about him at this point in the story?

In nature, things are neither good nor bad. Animals, plants, landscapes and weather have no connection with morality but humans are portrayed by Hill as essentially spiritual beings governed by consciences and predisposed to an awareness of the supernatural. This is certainly what happens to Kipps on his last night at Eel Marsh House.

Text **focus**

Re-read the text from the last paragraph on page 114 to the end of the chapter.
- Note the fear in the behaviour of Spider. Animals' senses of hearing and smell are more acute than those of humans.
- The bumping sound turns out to be made by the rocking chair on the wooden floor but inanimate objects do not move on their own.
- Note the locked door that doesn't have any visible locking mechanism.
- On page 117 the same locked door is suddenly open.

- The ghostly clip clop of the pony's hooves builds up to a crescendo culminating in the screams of a drowning child.
- The build up of supernatural happenings spills over into the next chapter. The climax, that is the highest point of Kipps' realisation and experience of the supernatural, is on pages 124 and 125. Re-read these pages and note that it is Spider's distress that makes Kipps pull himself together.

Sleep

It is worth noting that on his first night in Crythin Gifford, Arthur Kipps has the best night's sleep in memory but after the woman in black appears, his whole being, physical and mental, is disturbed for ever. Sleep is considered completely natural and is a theme that is explored in many texts, one that most GCSE students may be aware of is Shakespeare's *Macbeth*.

Sleep is mentioned in almost every chapter. Arthur Kipps is disturbed by dreams. The woman in black enters his dreams and haunts him. This blurs Kipps' sense of reality. It is widely believed that sleep deprivation can drive human beings mad. Also, sleep is linked metaphorically with death. These are interesting comparisons.

> **Pause for thought**
>
> It is worth highlighting references to sleep throughout the text. Look at the number of times Hill refers to sleep. Consider its importance at different times in the novel. Is sleep mentioned in conjunction with characters other than Kipps? Could this be significant in any way?

Childhood

Another recurring theme is that of childhood. As readers, we are acquainted with Nathaniel Pierston, Joseph Arthur Samuel Kipps and the children who line up at the school railings watching Alice Drablow's funeral. The juxtaposition (placing opposites next to each other) of the children and the appearance of the ghost is interesting as, usually, children symbolise innocence. It is particularly disconcerting that when Kipps smiles at one of the children the child does not smile back. At the time of first reading, the audience is not aware that the children of the village probably know the background to the woman in black so the dramatic irony is lost unless the book is studied carefully. Once you have read the

James Stellos in the Utah Shakespearean Festival's 2009 production of *The Woman in Black* (photo by Karl Hugh)

Utah Shakespearean Festival

Pause for thought

Study the text at the top of page 51. What evidence can you find which may suggest that these are not real children?

whole text, you may believe another interpretation of this which is that these children are the ghosts of the many children who have died due to the woman in black seeking her revenge.

The chapter on the nursery is a very telling one for portraying the theme of childhood. Mystery surrounds the room. The door has no visible locks when locked or when open. Kipps is so immersed in the supernatural world by this stage that he is prepared to believe anything he might see.

When Kipps discovers the source of the bumping noise, it is soon after he experiences the distressing sounds of the child drowning in the marshes. This has a profound effect on him and seeing Spider's distress, he comforts her as a mother would a child. Ironically, he himself is comforted by what he now recognises as the bumping sound of the moving rocking chair to such an extent he is almost transported back to his own childhood. The nursery represents the safety of childhood, the comfort of a mother or a nurse. Clearly, either supernatural influences or Kipps' vivid imagination are at work as the nursery does not have the abandoned atmosphere of the rest of the house. It is like a living museum commemorating a childhood 60 years before. Yet Kipps ceases to be afraid and for a while he becomes the protected innocent on his journey to discovery once more.

By placing the episode where the angry Kipps (who is outside searching for tools to break down the nursery door) experiences most vividly the sounds of the drowning child next to the episode in the nursery, Susan Hill is exploiting the contrasts between evil and goodness, evil and innocence and danger and safety. The confusion between Kipps' memories of his own nursery and the one in Eel Marsh House builds up the fear and the tension, only for it to be released by an overwhelming sense of sadness and loss leaving him drained and exhausted.

Review your learning

(Answers given on p. 89)

1 Who says 'innocence, once lost, is lost for ever' and what does he mean?

2 What does 'juxtaposition' mean and why do you think the author would use it?

More interactive questions and answers online.

Grade *booster*

A and A* candidates will be able to select textual evidence of the juxtaposition of the natural elements and supernatural activity and be able to comment intelligently on the effectiveness of this technique.

Style

- **What does the term 'style' refer to?**
- **How does Hill use settings?**
- **How does Hill make descriptions effective?**
- **For what purpose does Hill include dialogue?**
- **What viewpoint does Hill adopt?**
- **How does Hill use imagery and symbolism?**

Anyone who has read *The Woman in Black* will be able to retell the story, but you as a serious student and literary critic will earn no marks in the exam for doing this. Many exam questions relate to character and characterisation and most candidates will be able to write about them and their role in the novel. Writing about the author's style, however, is more complex but if you do this well you show the examiner that you have a sophisticated grasp of the book.

When you write about style you demonstrate that you understand the novel as a construct — that is, it has been 'built' by the author by putting together 'ingredients' in a certain way. Your job as literary critic is to 'un-pick' the novel to show how it has been constructed. You can compare yourself with an intelligent child who has a new toy. Have you noticed that the first thing a clever child does is to take the toy apart and put it together again to see how it works? This is what you do in your essay as you are looking at the choices Susan Hill has made and how she put her novel together.

Sometimes writers adopt a certain style that has been tried and tested. They are writing in a certain **genre** (this is a French word meaning 'type') in this instance a ghost story. Susan Hill believed the classic ghost story was being neglected in favour of the horror genre and wished to revive it. She researched other classic ghost stories and incorporated many of the conventions.

The list below gives some of the main features covered by the word 'style' and Susan Hill has made choices about all of them:

- The viewpoint from which the story is told, especially whether it is third person (an onlooker telling the story) or first person (a person telling his or her own story).
- How the settings add to the story.
- How dialogue and conversation are used and how realistic they are in presenting characters.

- The order of events, which is very important as it moves the story along and highlights aspects of themes.
- Withholding information in order to create tension and atmosphere, for example Samuel Daily could have given Kipps the background to Alice Drablow's affairs on the train in Chapter 3 but Susan Hill chooses to divulge what he knows on page 150.
- The way the writer uses names in the novel.
- How the writer uses imagery or word pictures to create descriptions and atmosphere.
- Symbolism.

Conventions of a ghost story

The Woman in Black follows in the tradition of the classic ghost story. Some famous ones are Charles Dickens' *A Christmas Carol* and *The Signalman*, Henry James' *The Turn of the Screw* and Edith Wharton's *Mr Jones* and *All Souls*. A ghost story is not the same as a horror story although the plot builds up to a horrific climax which is intended to terrify the reader. Put simply, a ghost story needs a ghost, the spirit of a person who has died but has not left the earth. A horror story is based in reality. A ghost story can only be understood in terms of the supernatural.

A ghost story relies on atmosphere that is often conveyed through physical phenomena such as the weather, gothic buildings, vivid settings,

James Stellos and Katie Wackowski in the Utah Shakespearean Festival's 2009 production of *The Woman in Black* (photo by Karl Hugh)

Utah Shakespearean Festival

and on hints and half suggestions such as those made by the landlord in *A Woman in Black*. The writer's intention is primarily to chill the audience to the core and to make the reader realise that not everything can be explained by science. Hamlet says: 'There are more things in heaven and earth, Horatio, / Than are dreamt of in your philosophy'.

The one thing that human beings do not know is what happens when we die. Ghost stories feed that fascination with the after-life and very often, because of that, have a Christian moral.

Grade *booster*

Susan Hill has her own website: **www.susan-hill.com**. Surf the web and find out what you can about her intentions and how she came to write *The Woman in Black*. You can ask her questions about the novel and what was in her mind when she wrote it. For example, the author of this study guide had difficulty tracing Kipps' journey from London via Crewe to Homerby and in locating Crythin Gifford. Susan Hill explained that Crythin Gifford was a fictional town and she imagined it somewhere on the east coast possibly as far north as the Holy Island of Lindisfarne or as far south as the Essex Marshes. In fact, she actually confessed that Crewe was put in to 'confuse and annoy'.

Pause for thought

You need to memorise the basic ingredients of a ghost story:
- a ghost
- an isolated haunted house
- extreme weather conditions
- a main character who doesn't believe in ghosts at the outset but changes when he has experienced the presence of one

This should help you understand how Susan Hill planned and structured her novel.

Viewpoint

The ghost story is told entirely by Arthur Kipps. This technique is known as a **first-person narrative**. The advantage of this technique is that it has a greater impact on the reader because it is immediate and realistic. Although in other contexts this technique can be restrictive, in this particular genre it is effective in that readers put themselves entirely in Kipps' position, seeing everything from his perspective and reliving his experiences. Although this limits the writer to presenting one point of view, Hill gets round this by reporting what others say and by using letters or correspondence such as those found by Kipps among Alice Drablow's papers.

When Kipps is going through Alice Drablow's papers, the reader can see events from different perspectives such as the prevailing attitudes of the time, Jennet Humfrye's distress and Alice Drablow's reluctance for the boy to have contact with her sister particularly as she had probably never bargained on the child growing to resemble his mother. Readers can also make their own judgement on the extent of Kipps' trauma from the way he

is looked after by Mr Bentley and from the length of time between Stella's death and his second marriage.

In effect, there are two Arthur Kipps in *The Woman in Black*: the retired old man and the eager young lawyer. We excuse many of the young man's imperfections such as his arrogance and his impatience because the older Kipps puts his youthful actions in context and this makes the reader believe in his judgement and his account of events.

Creating atmosphere: description of places and setting

The creation of atmosphere, character and most particularly a sense of place are the most important elements of a classic ghost story and Susan Hill recognises that these are her particular strengths as a writer. There are several locations for the action in the novel.

Monk's Piece

This is Arthur Kipps' home, a lonely house on a hill. Monk's Piece is a handsome, modest building on a grassy knoll at the end of a lane, next to a garden overlooking a meadow. (There is an orchard behind the house.) From one aspect can be seen farmland interspersed by woodland and from behind, rough scrub and heath land. It has an air of remoteness and isolation although it is only two miles from the village and seven miles from the nearest market town. Its very name suggests that Kipps has been living a quiet, hermit-like existence since coming here in his middle age and that he craves safety.

This place is presented in great detail in Chapter 1 and is useful for representing the normality of a happy family Christmas. The image of Isobel's three little boys asleep in bed on Christmas Eve while the adults gather round the roaring fire to tell stories can be compared to the preserved yet abandoned and later devastated nursery in Eel Marsh House.

The very name 'Monk's Piece' could be significant. Arthur Kipps retired here to live a life of reflection and the word 'piece' could be seen as a pun on the homophone 'peace'.

Mr Bentley's London chambers

This is a typical solicitor's office from where Kipps is sent on his mission. The premises are only mentioned briefly in the second chapter but are useful for creating atmosphere. The reader can picture Tomes with his runny nose incarcerated in his cubby hole surrounded by papers all linked in some way with death.

Crythin Gifford

Crythin Gifford is a market town near the east coast marshes where the funeral of Alice Drablow takes place. The very nature of this place is its remoteness and the fact that its inhabitants are inward looking. It is bleak and strange and the people 'tuck [themselves] in with [their] backs to the wind and carry on with [their] business' according to Samuel Daily (p. 39). This description immediately tells the reader that the people need to protect themselves but the question is, from what? The area of Crythin Gifford encompasses the following three places.

Eel Marsh House

This large lonely house near the coast, surrounded by marshland, is the home of Alice Drablow.

The Nine Lives Causeway

This is a treacherous raised by-way through the marshes from Crythin Gifford to Eel Marsh House.

Gapemouth Tunnel

This railway tunnel through the countryside separates the flatmarshes from the rest of the country. It could be seen as a symbolic passage from the real world into the realm of the supernatural. The very deliberate choice of names begins to establish the air of mystery and suspense at this early stage in the story. In contrast, a London park — the place where the woman in black takes her final revenge — is not given a name, possibly because the action in this part is horrific enough to speak for itself and also because the matter-of-fact way Kipps completes his story depicts his exhaustion. However, the reader can see another symbolic road: the great avenue of horse chestnut trees which like the Nine Lives Causeway turns out to be a passage from one life to another. It is by travelling down this avenue in a pony trap that Stella and the child meet their deaths just as Nathaniel, Keckwick and Rose Judd met theirs over half a century earlier. Like Jennet Humfrye, Kipps is forced to witness the horrific death of his own child.

Creating atmosphere: the weather and the natural environment

The weather is a very important phenomenon when creating the atmosphere and when presenting the natural world. The reader is told from the outset that the weather is very important to Kipps. He states 'My

spirits have for many years now been excessively affected by the ways of the weather...' (p. 10, l. 7).

Christmas Eve is clear and frosty and Kipps feels contented. The day he set eyes on Monk's Piece for the first time, he remarked to Mr Bentley on the 'calm and sweetness of the day'. This was clearly a good omen, for his life here is safe and calm. In contrast, the journey to Crythin Gifford is dogged by a pea-souper: '...a yellow fog, a filthy, evil-smelling fog, a fog that choked and blinded, smeared and stained' (p. 25, l. 13).

It is also described as 'menacing and sinister'. It is under these conditions that Kipps begins his journey. The description of the lights of shops, the braziers of road menders, their cauldrons of pungent tar and the lamp-lighter's lanterns are reminiscent of hell. This foreshadows the dangers of his mission.

Even before Kipps embarks on his journey, the fog shrouds the truth. When Mr Bentley inadvertently tries to clear the window, while pondering the question whether or not Alice Drablow had children, 'the fog loomed yellow-grey and thicker than ever'. This signifies the deepening of the mystery. Despite his negative reply and the long considered pause, it suggests that he knew she did have a child, an adopted son — Nathaniel Pierston. Nevertheless, whether or not he is part of the conspiracy of silence is never established but it may go some way to explain why Mr Bentley felt responsible for what happened to Kipps.

The literary tradition of the weather heralding events of the plot is a well-established one. The term 'pathetic fallacy' was coined by a great writer called Ruskin to describe it. Throughout the novel, sea frets or mists shroud events, great gales and howling winds add to Kipps' fears when he is marooned at Eel Marsh House. Hill builds and releases tension through the use of pathetic fallacy, for example in the chapter 'In the Nursery' the bright crisp autumn day symbolises Kipps' optimism but the reader knows that when the wind drops and darkness falls dramatic events will follow. Spider the dog picks up on the tension before Kipps.

The tension is then further increased by the bumping sound, and reaches a climax at the ghostly sounds of the pony and trap and child sinking in the marshes.

In the next chapter, 'Whistle and I'll Come to You', Susan Hill uses the wind and darkness to similar effect: '...hearing the wind rage round like a lion, howling at the doors and beating upon windows...' (p. 123, l. 18).

Another image connects the weather with the supernatural 'the tumult of the wind, like a banshee'. A **banshee** is an Irish term for a female ghost who heralds the death of an important person. She is either depicted as an

> **Key quotation**
>
> ...Spider began to whine, a thin, pitiful frightened moan...My throat felt constricted and dry and I had begun to shiver.
>
> (p. 109, l. 22)

old hag or a beautiful woman. She is known as 'a woman of the side' or 'a bystander'. This has a clear connection with the woman in black. Here, Susan Hill combines pathetic fallacy with symbolism and use of similes. It is almost impossible to separate these elements of Hill's style because it is the way in which they interweave that makes her creation of atmosphere so effective.

Imagery and the writer's use of language

The term **imagery** refers to the kind of pictures or images the writer's words create in the mind of the reader. It covers specific terms such as metaphor, simile and personification.

A **metaphor** is used to describe something in terms of something else, for example on page 34, line 5 'that great cavern of a railway station' is saying that King's Cross Station *is* an enormous cave.

A **simile** is used to describe something by saying it is *like* something else. It is always easy to recognise because the actual phrase must contain either the word *like* or the word *as*. For example page 34, line 6, '[the railway station was] glowing like the interior of a black-smith's forge'.

Personification is the name given to attributing human qualities to something inanimate: 'The wind will blow itself out and take the rain off with it by morning,' says Samuel Daily in a matter of fact way, making the wind and the rain sound like a human couple (p. 35, l. 28).

Susan Hill uses imagery to build tension and suspense into the atmosphere particularly with reference to the weather. On page 36 she describes the bursts of rain 'like sprays of light artillery fire, upon the windows' as if the country were at war. On page 49 she describes the woman in black as a 'victim of starvation'.

There are several examples of the use of imagery on almost every page of the story. Which of them you choose to comment on will depend on your purpose and the essay task you are addressing. It is important that you do comment on the imagery and the writer's use of language because they form part of the assessment objectives on which you are being examined. In order to do this effectively you should develop the skill of embedding quotations (see p. 69) and remember to comment on individual words — the pictures they create as well as the sound they make. Remember to write a lot about a little — it is better (and easier) to write about individual words or very short phrases than large chunks of text or even whole sentences. You can pick out individual words such as vivid

(see p. 69)

> **Pause for thought**
>
> Think about the idea of the battle between good and evil. Could this be foreshadowing of the idea of the innocent Kipps going unarmed on a journey of discovery?

> **Grade *booster***
>
> To gain a grade C or above, examiners need to see that you can comment on writers' use of language effectively. Don't forget to comment on the effects created by the use of short sentences, repetition, questions, monosyllabic words and harsh consonant sounds which add a sense of fear, danger or anger.

verbs, effectively used adjectives and adverbs to show how readers' feelings are being manipulated by the writer. Certain words may be especially effective in creating atmosphere and evoking fear, sadness and so on.

Dialogue

Although there are many advantages in using the first-person narrative, the one disadvantage is that it is limiting the reader to the viewpoint of Arthur Kipps. One of the ways in which Susan Hill gets around this problem is through using dialogue. This is particularly useful in helping establish characters by the way they speak. For example, Susan Hill (or Kipps) does not say that Mr Bentley is a ponderous, eccentric old man who fraternises with the aristocracy but instead has him say to Kipps when pondering his reasons for not attending Arthur Daily's funeral personally: 'And, then, there's the chance that Lord Boltrope will need to see me. I ought to be here, do you see?' (p. 30, l. 20). In this way, Mr Bentley is brought to life.

The dialogue in 'Mr Jerome is Afraid' is used in a different way. The conversation between the young Kipps and Jerome is written in direct speech interspersed with commentary by the older Kipps who tells the story. This gives the reader a perspective on Jerome's fear and young Kipps' impatience. Jerome's terror seems to feed young Kipps' bravado. 'And I doubt if the woman in black can have any animosity towards *me*. I wonder who she was. *Is?* I laughed though it came out sounding quite false into the room' (p. 90, l. 13).

Dialogue is also used for a significant purpose in 'A Packet of Letters'. Kipps pieces together the information about the background of the woman in black from Alice

Dan Kremer and James Stellos in the Utah Shakespearean Festival's 2009 production of *The Woman in Black* (photo by Karl Hugh)

Drablow's papers and the revelations are significant. To slow down the pace of the narrative, Susan Hill has Kipps discuss his findings with Samuel Daily using dialogue for the purpose of fitting the final pieces of the puzzle together and helping the reader absorb the information. However, the greatest significance of this particular piece of dialogue is for Daily to present slowly the final horror in the form of a climax. 'And whenever she has been seen…in the graveyard, on the marsh, in the streets of the town…in some violent or dreadful circumstance, a child has died' (p. 149, l. 22).

In this way, Hill attempts to reproduce the pace at which the significance of this information sinks into Kipps' brain and to have maximum impact on the reader.

Text focus

Read page 145 from line 4 to page 150 line 14.
- Notice the balance between amount of narrative and the amount of dialogue.
- Notice how much is revealed by the words of the characters.
- Notice how much is revealed by the pauses and the gestures of the characters.
- Look at the types of sentences and the use of questions, and the way the writer italicises some words for emphasis.

Symbolism

Imagery is often linked to symbolism and the most common use of symbolism in _The Woman in Black_ is connected with death. A symbol is a recurring image which is used by the writer to represent something else. We associate some things subconsciously with events which frighten us, for example the very title, _The Woman in Black,_ may make us think of death, as traditionally in western culture, black is worn to funerals. Ravens are black birds also associated with death and yew trees are the

Katie Wackowski and James Stellos in the Utah Shakespearean Festival's 2009 production of _The Woman in Black_ (photo by Karl Hugh)

Utah Shakespearean Festival

most common type of tree found in graveyards. Kipps uses the metaphor 'our appearance…was that of a pair of gloomy ravens' to describe himself and Jerome at Alice Drablow's funeral (p. 46). The bell ringing on page 29 — 'A church bell began to toll' — also is a symbol that heralds death. In addition, there was a blackbird singing its 'November song' in the graveyard.

Much of the action takes place in graveyards. The woman in black is first seen in the graveyard at Alice Drablow's funeral, she is next seen as a malevolent presence in the graveyard of the ruined monastery in the grounds of Eel Marsh House. Her arrival is heralded by the harsh croaking of an ugly satanic sea vulture. Whereas birds are used to symbolise death, other animals, like Spider the dog, represent safety and companionship. The pony is seen as 'solid' and dependable yet the recurring sound of the pony and trap links the present with the past. It is fitting that Kipps' son dies while being a passenger in a pony and trap just as the child of Jennet Humfrye did over half a century earlier.

All these events can be seen to be linked by symbols. Indeed the very names are symbolic. The Nine Lives Causeway may make us think about escaping or cheating death — a cat is said to have nine lives. Gapemouth Tunnel could symbolise entering the jaws of hell. Tomes is associated with all the huge ledgers and law books with which he works. Crythin Gifford could symbolise the noise of the easterly wind coming in off the sea. Mostly symbolism is used to exploit our fear of death and the supernatural as every classic ghost story should.

Review your learning

(Answers given on pp. 89–90)
1. What viewpoint does Susan Hill adopt?
2. Give an example of a metaphor, a simile, and personification used in this chapter of this guide. In your own words explain how each is effective.
3. Why is dialogue important?
4. What is the difference between imagery and symbolism?

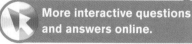
More interactive questions and answers online.

Tackling the exam

- How well do you know your text?
- What are tiers of entry?
- How should you plan and structure your exam essay?
- How should you provide evidence to support your interpretation of the text?

Knowing your text

Read your text several times and use this text guide to help you. You will notice different things on your second and third readings and begin to enjoy making connections you have never thought of before. You will be allowed to take your text into the examination but unless you are very familiar with it, it could become more of a hindrance than a help as you could waste a lot of time re-reading parts that you really should know.

Although you gain no marks for retelling the story you have to show the examiner you know it well. You should have a sound grasp of the following:

- the main sequence of events (the structure)
- the parts played by each of the characters
- the nature of the ghost story
- the writer's possible intentions

You need to learn the correct spellings of the names of people and places.

Higher and foundation tiers

You will be entered for the examination at either foundation or higher tier. Make sure you know your target grade. If you are a foundation candidate, your target is no higher than a C grade. If you are a higher candidate, your target can be as high as an A* grade but no lower than a D. If you do not achieve at least a D grade, you will not receive an award at all on the higher papers.

Foundation paper

Often, the questions on higher and foundation papers are similar, except that on the foundation tier you are given bullet points to help you. These

serve to give some broad structure to your essay, although they are often phrased as suggestions rather than instructions. Unless you work out a very clear structure of your own, it is advisable to follow them.

Below are some examples of foundation-type questions.

1 Write about two places in the novel where setting is important to the story.
- Describe these places and briefly say what happens in each of them.
- Say why they are important to the story, explain the atmosphere of each place and what the writer wants the reader to think and feel.
- Explain how successful she has been. Give reasons for your views.

2 Choose two of the following characters and write about their importance in the novel: Mr Bentley, Mr Samuel Daily, the landlord of the Gifford Arms, Keckwick.
- Write about their role in the novel, referring to what they say and do.
- Write about what Kipps thinks about them.
- Write about what you think about them and their role.

3 Why do you think Susan Hill called her story *The Woman in Black*? How effective is it as a title?
- Write about the appearance and the importance of the ghost in the story.
- Write about religious beliefs at the time.
- Explain your feelings about what she does and her intentions.

Higher paper

At the higher tier you are unlikely to be given bullet points to help you so it is a good idea to work out your own points before you start on a comprehensive plan. You need to think about what the question is asking you to do. You may be asked to write about themes or style, not just about character and setting. Examiners are especially keen to see how well you can comment on the language and structure of a text. You will only be given bullet points if the question is a difficult one.

Below are some examples of higher-type questions.

1 How does Susan Hill explore the theme of revenge in the novel? You should make detailed reference to Christian beliefs and moral attitudes of the time and the language used to express these ideas in the novel.

2 Should Jennet Humfrye be pitied or condemned? Explore her behaviour when she was alive and as a ghost.

3 Why do you think Susan Hill called her story *The Woman in Black*? How effective is it as a title?

The question

You will be given a choice of questions so obviously you choose the one that you can say most about. This is not necessarily the one that looks the easiest. Sometimes questions appear to be so simple you can't find enough to say to gain you high marks. Believe it or not, examiners are not out to trick you and they give a lot of time to setting questions that are straightforward and understandable. They want to give you marks for the things you say and they don't ever knock marks off. However, they can only award marks to relevant points and the development of these points. So, the message is, make sure you know what you are being asked to do. Underline the key words. Break down the task and plan carefully.

Breaking down the question

Here is a possible breakdown of a question without bullet points.

Consider Kipps' role in *A Woman in Black* and how effectively Hill portrays him.

- Kipps' role as the narrator. The effective use of the first person.
- How Susan Hill presents him as a young man.
- The contrast between the character of the young and middle-aged Kipps.
- The decisions he makes and how he reflects upon his own actions and character.
- His reactions to the events in the story.

Planning your answers

The section above already goes part of the way to breaking down and interpreting the question in preparation for forming your plan. If you are provided with bullet points, you can use them instead but, remember, you still have quite a lot of planning to do.

The form of your plan

You may find it helpful to use a mind map or diagram of some kind as it may help you to keep your mind open to new ideas as you plan so you can add to it at a later stage. Then you need to arrange them. Deciding on an order and numbering them will help.

Structuring your essay

Every essay must have:

1 an introduction
2 a development section
3 an effective ending

Introduction or beginning

Keep your introduction short and to the point. Start with a strong statement. For example:

Kipps has two important roles in *A Woman in Black*, the narrator and the main character.

Don't spend time explaining what you are going to do or what you intend to show. Refer to the key words of the question. For example:

In allowing Kipps to tell his own story in the first person Susan Hill allows him to have a more immediate effect on the reader. This is effective because it arouses sympathy and it is easier for the reader to identify with his situation as the story unfolds. However, there are occasions when she interrupts the narrative in order to slow down the pace of events and comment on the action.

Then move on to the development of the essay.

Development or the middle

The success of this part of the essay depends on how well you have prepared your plan. You have jotted down notes on what you are going to say and the order in which you are going to make your points. Now the challenge is to put them together so the ideas flow smoothly. To do this, you need practice using discourse markers (words which link ideas). Here are some examples:

- 'First' or 'primarily' signpost your main point.
- 'Furthermore' or 'in addition to' indicate that another point is being made.
- 'However' signposts an exception.
- 'Nevertheless', 'nonetheless' and 'despite this' mean you are going to consider alternative interpretations.
- 'Another example' means you are developing the idea further.
- 'Moreover' signals that a more decisive point is about to be made.
- 'Lastly', 'finally' or 'in conclusion' show you are coming to the end.

Conclusion or end

Your conclusion should draw all your arguments to a logical ending. Don't simply repeat your ideas. Refer back to the key words in the question and try to give an overview and a personal response. A good technique is to choose an apt quotation from the text. There are many ways you could use the last line from *The Woman in Black* because it illustrates so many points in the story, for example Kipps' exhausted state of mind or Susan Hill's narrative technique.

Using quotations and referring to text

It is essential to use quotations and references to the text in your exam essay. This is to provide evidence for the points you make and to show that you know the text. You are expected to express your personal views and interpretations of what the writer may be saying. The examiner will be delighted if you say something original. However, you must always back up your views with evidence.

Separate quotations

The first kind of quotation you can use is a separate quotation. This means making your point then backing it up with a quotation. Remember to begin quotations which are longer than three words on a separate line. For example:

Hill describes the way the filthy fog permeates every aspect of life. This is a really disgusting simile:

[the fog] '...seething through cracks and crannies like sour breath,'

Embedded quotations

An embedded quotation is one which runs on from your own words on the same line or is included within the sentence you are writing. Embedded quotations are considered more sophisticated and you will be rewarded if you use them correctly within grammatically correct sentences. Don't forget to put quotation marks in the correct place. For example:

The older Kipps looks back at his own 'priggish' behaviour as a young man ...

Referring to the text

It is not always necessary to use a quotation. If you cannot accurately recall or find the quotation you want easily, it is often just as good to refer to it. For example, you could write:

Kipps refers to the way Londoners look down on people from the provinces.

Referring to the author and title

You can refer to Susan Hill by her surname only or as the author. You can also save time by using a simplification of the book's title. Give the title in full the first time you use it, for example 'The Woman in Black (TWiB)'. You can then use TWiB on its own in the rest of your answer.

Writing in the appropriate style

Remember you are expected to write in an appropriate style for a formal examination essay. You must write in an appropriate register. This means:

- not using colloquial language or slang unless using a direct quotation from the text, in which case remember to use quotation marks. For example, 'The young Arthur Kipps is a bit of a posh twit who thinks he's better than the people of Crythin Gifford' is definitely written in an inappropriate style
- not becoming too personal, for example, 'Mr Bentley reminds me of my doctor because...'
- using suitable phrases for an academic essay. For example it is better to say 'It could be argued that...' not 'I reckon that...'

Writing in the first person

Although this style has become more common, try not to use it. If you do, you are unlikely to achieve the highest grades.

Review your learning

(Answers given on p. 90)
1. Name two ways of using quotations.
2. What is a discourse marker?
3. Give two pieces of advice on how to start an answer.
4. What is the point of a conclusion?
5. Should you write in the first person?

 More interactive questions and answers online.

Assessment Objectives and skills

- How will your essay be marked?
- What are the Assessment Objectives?
- How do the Assessment Objectives apply to different exam boards?
- What skills are you required to show?
- How can you gain extra marks related to each Assessment Objective?
- Improving your grade
- What will turn a C essay into an A* essay?

An examiner marking your exam essay will be trying to give you marks, but will only be able to do so if you succeed in fulfilling the key Assessment Objectives (AOs) for English literature.

The AOs that you will be assessed on are:

- AO1: respond to texts critically and imaginatively; select and evaluate relevant textual detail to illustrate and support interpretations.
- AO2: explain how language, structure and form contribute to writers' presentation of ideas, themes and settings.
- AO4: relate texts to their social, cultural and historical contexts; explain how texts have been influential and significant to self and other readers in different contexts and at different times.

Breaking down the Assessment Objectives

AO1

Respond to texts critically and imaginatively; select and evaluate relevant textual detail to illustrate and support interpretations.

This means you have to say what you think of the story and why. You have to use your imagination and be able to empathise with characters and their situation. You have to evaluate, which involves realising that the

author has made choices and giving your views on how effective these choices are. For example, Susan Hill has chosen not to develop many of the characters, especially the women. This shows the relative unimportance of women at the time. You also have to use quotations to back up your interpretation.

AO2

Explain how language, structure and form contribute to writers' presentation of ideas, themes and settings.

The word **language** refers to how the author uses words for effect. For example, you must be able to pick out effective words and phrases to show how Hill creates atmosphere. This involves:

- the use of sounds — alliteration, onomatopoeia and assonance, although there is no need to remember these terms if you find it difficult
- imagery — simile and metaphor, these terms you should know and be able to use
- words that appeal to the five senses — these are used to evoke particular feelings in the reader

The word **structure** refers to the overall shape of the story. The introduction of *The Woman in Black* is set 30 years after the main events. The subsequent chapters tell the main story and the end of the final chapter returns back to the time of the introduction.

The word **form** in this case refers to the genre. *The Woman in Black* has all the conventional ingredients of a ghost story.

There are separate sections on **theme** and **settings** in this guide.

AO4

Relate texts to their social, cultural and historical contexts; explain how texts have been influential and significant to self and other readers in different contexts and at different times.

Relate texts to their social, cultural and historical contexts — you have to show appreciation of the ideas, beliefs, attitudes and values of people in the time the story was set (1850s up to the 1930s). For example, people had stricter moral and religious values. Sex outside marriage was taboo. Christianity was the prevailing religion: most people went to church and believed in an after-life; therefore the older people generally accepted that disturbed spirits wandered the earth. Younger people, on the whole, were more sceptical as they relied on reason and science and mocked superstition — that is until they came upon phenomena they could not explain.

Explain how texts have been influential and significant to self and other readers in different contexts and at different times — there is some overlap here with the first part of AO4, though here the emphasis is on personal response. You need to show awareness of Susan Hill's wish to revive the art form of telling ghost stories as Hollywood was becoming more influential and horror and thriller genres appeared to be taking over. Contemporary readers may bring different beliefs and attitudes to the text. Britain has become more multicultural and multi-religious. Some traditionalists would say that strict observance of Christian religious beliefs and practices has declined as people have become more liberal and are no longer subservient to people of a higher social status.

Unless you can understand that your own beliefs and attitudes are based on contemporary influences you are unlikely to appreciate the ghost story fully. In other words, you don't have to believe in ghosts but you have to understand why the characters in *The Woman in Black* did.

Quality of Written Communication (QWC)

- Ensure that text is legible and that spelling, punctuation and grammar are accurate so that your meaning is clear.
- Select and use a form and style of writing appropriate to purpose and to complex subject matter.
- Organise information clearly and coherently, using specialist vocabulary when relevant.

> **Pause for thought**
>
> These points apply to all your examinations, not just English literature.

These objectives are straightforward. They mean you should:

1 Make sure the examiner can read your handwriting. Use correct spellings and punctuation and make sure your sentences make sense
2 Use standard English; no slang and no swear words. Avoid colloquial expressions and clichés. Adopt a formal academic tone

What you will *not* get marks for

- Attempting to write all you know about the story — this is not really possible unless you know very little and it won't impress the examiner, so answer the question.
- Retelling the story — this is a key feature of answers in the lowest grade band so don't do it. The best way is to highlight the key words in the question and make sure you use at least some of them in every paragraph. This helps you focus on the question.
- Using very long quotations — it is a waste of time, you are not showing the examiner your work and you'll lose sight of the point you are trying to make. One word or short phrases are most effective.

- Using technical terms like alliteration or onomatopoeia without explaining the effect on the reader — you don't gain marks for just identifying features without saying how and why they are used.

The AQA examination

You will be answering one question on *The Woman in Black* from a choice of two in the Paper 1, Section A, Modern Prose Section of the literature examination. It is worth 20% of your total grade and is marked out of 30 marks. You will be able to take a clean copy of the text into the examination with you. 'Clean' means without notes, annotations, highlights, underlining, turned-over pages, post-it notes, paper clips or any other devices which may help you save time or aid you in any way in preparing your answers. You should complete your answer in 45 minutes; if you don't you will not have enough time to complete the 'Exploring Cultures' section.

Your essay will then be awarded a mark from one of six bands (the first three are printed here) depending on which criteria the examiner judges that it best fits.

Mark band 6 (26–30 marks)

Candidates demonstrate:

- insightful/exploratory response to text
- close analysis of detail to support interpretation
- evaluation of writer's uses of language and/or form and/or structure and effect on readers/audience
- convincing/imaginative interpretation of ideas/themes/settings

Information is presented in a way which assists with communication of meaning.

Syntax and spelling are generally accurate.

Mark band 5 (21–25 marks)

Candidates demonstrate:

- exploratory response to text
- analytical use of details to support interpretation
- analysis of writer's uses of language and/or structure and/or form
- exploration of themes/ideas/settings

Information is usually presented in a way which assists with communication of meaning.

Syntax and spelling are generally accurate.

Mark band 4 (16–20 marks)

Candidates demonstrate:

- considered/qualified response to text
- details linked to interpretation
- appreciation/consideration of writer's use of language and/or form and/or structure and effect on readers/audience
- thoughtful consideration of ideas/themes/settings

Information is presented in a way which is generally clear. Syntax and spelling have some degree of accuracy.

Marks and grades

AQA no longer links marks to grades. However, it is not difficult to work out that you must achieve a mark near the top of band 6 to achieve an A* grade and a mark at the upper/middle of band 4 to achieve a C grade.

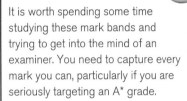

Pause for thought

It is worth spending some time studying these mark bands and trying to get into the mind of an examiner. You need to capture every mark you can, particularly if you are seriously targeting an A* grade.

Review your learning

(Answers given on p. 90)

1. Make a list of things you must *not* do when tackling your question.
2. What is the first thing you should do when you have chosen the question you want to answer?
3. How long do you have to complete the question on this text?
4. What are Assessment Objectives?
5. What must you mention in the opening paragraph?

More interactive questions and answers online.

Sample essays

Four sample essays are provided below — C-grade and A*-grade answers to two different types of questions: a character-based question and a theme-based question. It is suggested that you read the C-grade essays first and see how you could improve upon them. Then read the A*-grade essays. However, remember that there could be many different but equally good approaches to the same essay. These sample essays are not meant to be learned and reproduced in the exam.

Question 1

Write about two episodes in the novel that you think are frightening.
Write about:
- what happens
- the techniques used by Hill to frighten the reader
- why you think these events are important

C-grade essay

1 Addresses the question straight away. Short introduction

The two events that I think are most frightening are when Spider is lured into the marshes and nearly dies and the death of Kipps' son at the end of his story.**1**

In the first episode Kipps is woken up by the dog scratching and whining at the door asking to be let out. It is really cold outside and Kipps waits impatiently while the dog goes to the toilet in the long grass. This is quite a normal start to Kipps' day. Then he hears a commanding whistle and the dog shoots off. Susan Hill uses a metaphor here to show how fast Spider ran 'as though after a hare' and then a pattern of three to show how quickly it ran into the dangerous wet marshes.**2**

2 Identifies the purpose of writer's use of language but does not explore effect

It is really frightening because Kipps says it wasn't a trick of the wind, it was a real whistle but he says it didn't come from any human lips. This suggests it is supernatural.**3** This fits in with the title of the chapter which Hill pinched from another ghost story by M. R. James.

3 Shows awareness of theme

4 Begins to explore the effect of the language chosen by the writer

Some words used to stress the fear are 'horror' 'floundering' and 'yelping'. These show how fast Spider is sinking. Hill uses alliteration to show how much Kipps loved the little dog:**4**

'…the brave bright little creature who had given me such consolation and cheer in that desperate spot.'**5**

This episode is really scary because you think the dog is going to die and Kipps might as well but really you know Kipps won't because he is telling the story.**6** Anyway after a really long struggle Kipps manages to pull Spider out and just when you think everything is alright, Kipps sees the woman in black staring at them from the nursery window. This is really scary, so scary that Kipps passes out!**7**

At the beginning of the second episode**8** Susan Hill chooses a nice sunny day when Arthur, his wife Stella and baby Joseph Arthur Samuel are in the park in London. The baby doesn't like the donkey ride so Stella takes him on a ride in a pony and trap. This might be a warning or foreshadowing**9** because remember Jennet Humfrye's son died in a pony and trap on the marshes nearly 50 years ago. It is even more frightening because Kipps sees her ghost just before this and he believed that once he had left Crythin Gifford he was safe.

Suddenly the woman in black jumps out from behind a tree and scares the horse which rears and smashes the cart against the tree. Stella is badly injured and dies later but Joseph the baby dies instantly. This is at the end of Kipps' story.**10** It is a horrible ending and really scares the reader because the story stops there as if Kipps can't go on telling it. This makes the reader feel really sorry for him.**11**

A*-grade essay

Fear is a central theme in Hill's ghost story and there are several episodes which illustrate this. The two most poignant and frightening are the death of Kipps' baby son and the night after Kipps is allowed into the nursery at Eel Marsh House.**1** These are very different episodes because in fact nothing happens in the latter other than Kipps is woken by the storm and hears 'the familiar cry of desperation and anguish, a cry for help from a child somewhere out on the marsh'**2** which he knows has no foundation in reality. Yet in the episode at the end of his account his baby son is killed.

In the first episode Kipps is awoken by the storm. Hill uses a simile to describe his immediate feelings of danger and uncertainty:

'The house felt like a ship at sea, battered by the gale that came roaring across the open marsh.'

The words 'battered' 'roaring' and 'open' emphasise Kipps' vulnerability and exposure to the elements. The sound of these words is harsh and frightening and Kipps feels 'like a small boy again.'**3** His fear increases as he hears the ghostly cry of a child in danger. He goes out onto the landing, a 'tremendous blast of wind' rocks the house and the lights went out. This reminds me of a gothic horror

5 Uses quotation to support viewpoint

6 Is aware that the story is a construction

7 Begins to make some very valid literary comments but the style is too colloquial

8 Moves on to the second episode

9 Recognises another literary technique and is able to make cross-references with other parts of the text

10 Succinct style in describing what happened in the episode

11 Personal response to the ending

1 Considered qualified response to the text

2 Skilful use of embedded quotation

3 Appreciation of writer's use of language

movie as in those days they wouldn't have had electricity but paraffin lamps and for them all to go out together has got to be more than a coincidence.**4** Susan Hill maintains the tension and builds up the fear. Kipps panics as he has left his torch on the bedside table. He senses the presence of another person passing by him and begins to 'doubt his own reality'. He is desperate for light and goes back to his room to collect his torch. By using fine detail, Hill increases the fear until finally he reaches the torch, falls over the dog and the torch smashes onto the floor! He is so terrified he is on the verge of 'weeping tears of despair and fear'. Instead he expresses his fear through rage and thumps the floor.

Eventually Kipps' fear subsides as he sits on the floor and cuddles Spider, he feels calmer although the wind howls around him and the sound of the child plays over and over in his brain. At this point the tension is relieved. Susan Hill slows down the pace of the narrative by including fine detail. Kipps eventually gets up and lights a candle. In the candlelight he begins to recover as he rationalises

that he was paralysed by his fear.**5** Hill cleverly points out the ways in which this episode could have ended by presenting Kipps' own thoughts about human reactions. He believes that when pushed to the limits, a man cannot maintain a state of heightened emotion. He either runs away and goes mad or gradually comes to his senses and restores his normal state of mind. In this way Hill enters

the story using Kipps to express her own views and this serves to relax the tension and is a clever way of using anti-climax.**6** After this nothing happened. There were no other strange and dreadful happenings that night and as Kipps lies in bed his fear is replaced by 'an overwhelming grief and sadness'.

The second episode is more horrific though less frightening. Whereas in the first episode Hill creates a fearful atmosphere by using a violent storm (the wind and the darkness exacerbate Kipps' feeling of terror and panic) here she uses the opposite technique in setting her scene on a pleasant, summer's afternoon in a London park. There are plenty of people about and 'a festive, holiday air about

the place'.**7** Instead of a lonely man in an isolated house weathering a storm in the dead of night, she creates a relaxed setting using boats on a lake, a brass band playing 'jolly tunes' and ice-cream stalls. Kipps and Stella are proudly

observing baby Joseph attempting to walk in the sunshine.**8**

In contrast to building tension by degrees, in this episode Hill uses shock tactics. Stella and Joseph take a ride in a pony and trap. This is a good example of fore-

shadowing.**9**

'And then, quite suddenly, I saw her.'

The readers do not need to be told who, they know!**10** Hill's clever use of commas in this sentence chills the spine. We know the child will die.**11** Kipps describes his own feelings of 'incredulity...astonishment...cold fear'.

He is paralysed and overwhelmed by darkness although his surroundings don't change. The tension is broken when Stella and the baby come into sight. The baby is 'waving his little arms in delight'. Then almost in slow motion the woman in black reveals herself from behind a tree, the horse bolts and careers through the glade and hits 'a huge tree trunk', the baby is thrown clear (relief) against another tree. The irony here is sickening.**12** Kipps can no longer continue with the story. Seven lines later he ends it with the word 'Enough'.

12 Sophisticated personal response

The fear in the first episode is much more sustained and created in a very traditional way using pathetic fallacy, fine detail and strong emotive vocabulary. In contrast the episode where the baby is killed is shocking and horrific. The fear doesn't go away. The reader is left to decide which path this man Kipps followed after this. Did he run away and go mad? Or did he gradually come to his senses and resume a normal life? The story has come full circle.**13** We know that it took Kipps 13 years to recover to some state of normality but it could be argued that he is still haunted by the terrible memories and that is why in an effort to purge his life of fear he felt compelled to write his story.**14**

13 Considered, qualified response to the text

14 Flawless syntax and spelling

Question 2

Arthur Kipps is both the narrator and a central character in the ghost story. How does he change from the young lawyer about to travel to Crythin Gifford to the middle-aged step-father who feels compelled to write his story?

C-grade essay

Arthur Kipps' character**1** changes greatly in the novel. In the main story he is a typical young man. He is a middle-class, trainee lawyer who is well educated and clever. When he is sent to Crythin Gifford he is glad to have something interesting to do, it is like an adventure, he is not stuck in an office doing boring paperwork. He is impatient because Mr Bentley is so slow in giving him instructions.**2**

1 Key word identified

2 Brief introductory paragraph

When he is on the train he feels really important and to begin with he shows off to Samuel daily then gets tiered of him.**3**

3 Spelling and punctuation errors

'In my youthful and priggish way, summed up and all but dismissed him.'

We wouldn't use the word 'priggish' now because it is pompous, posh and old-fashioned.**4**

4 Aware of language changing over time and social and historical implications

On arriving at the Gifford Arms, Kipps treats the landlord in much the same way. Kipps is a Londoner who thinks he is better than 'primitive'**5** people in the rest of the country but the landlord annoys him because he ignores his questions. At

5 Embeds quotations with ease

6 Insight into character

7 Understands the use of repetition and is aware of structure

8 Remains focused on the question

9 Although there is some valid comment there is also a tendency to lapse into regurgitating narrative here

10 Relevant detail to support viewpoint

11 Understands theme

this point in the story Kipps has no worries he just wants to do his job well, gain promotion and go back to Stella, his fiancée in London. He sleeps easy at night.**6**

This all changes when he sees the woman in black and realises she is a ghost. He keeps repeating 'I did not believe in ghosts'. This suggests that he does now and something really bad happened to make him change his mind. This is called foreshadowing because Susan Hill is preparing the reader for what happens next.**7**

Lots of bad things happen to Kipps in Crythin Gifford. He hears the sound of a child drowning in the marshes, and the ghostly sounds of a pony and trap sinking. He is alone and the weather is stormy. Susan Hill uses some great sounds of the wind and the rain to create a really frightening atmosphere and Kipps begins to have nightmares.

This changes him.**8** He keeps seeing the ghost who:

'...directed the purest hatred and loathing with all the force that was available to her,'

and he is filled with fear.

From that moment all his reasoning and logic go out the window. He gradually becomes a nervous wreck and when Spider is lured by the ghostly whistle into the marshes and nearly dies he has to get out of Eel Marsh House. When he learns the whole background to the woman in black he has a nervous breakdown and Stella has to come and take him back to London. For a time he recovers but when the woman in black appears for the final time in the London park and causes the death of his wife and child he becomes a complete wreck. The main story ends here.**9**

The first chapter shows what Kipps was like as an old man. It took him years to recover and he is a completely different character. It is like he had all the stuffing knocked out of him. He wants a quiet life in the country. He collects watercolours, he smokes a pipe and he is alarmed when his step-sons start telling silly ghost stories because it reminds him of that terrible time in his life. He hasn't even told his wife what happened. He has kept this secret for 30 years and feels it's time to write down his story because once it is out in the open then he might start to deal with it properly.**10**

However at Christmas he feels safe because Christians believe God won't let evil spirits enter their souls.**11**

'Tomorrow was Christmas Day, and I looked forward to it eagerly and with gladness, it would be a time of family joy and merrymaking, love and friendship, fun and laughter.

When it was over I would have work to do.'

Through his life Kipps has suffered from a lot of mental illness and only got through it with the help of good friends like his wife and step-family and Mr Bentley. It changed him from being very confident and ambitious into an old man who just wanted a quiet life in the countryside.**12**

12 A simple but effective concluding paragraph

A*-grade essay

Susan Hill's technique which allows the main character to tell his story is most effective because he reveals his character through his words and actions. He is aware of his shortcomings as a young man and reflects on his own actions. By presenting Kipps in this way the reader can identify with his experiences and share his fears and emotions as a terrible period in his life is relived.**1**

1 Aware of the story as a construction: characterisation not character

In the first chapter Kipps appears to have everything a middle-aged man could want — a happy family, a beautiful house, a 'dear wife' and plenty of money. This is illustrated at Christmastime in order to exaggerate his domestic bliss. This is in contrast to a period 16 years earlier when he was 'prone to nervous illnesses and conditions' as a result of experiences [he] 'is going to relate'.**2** Kipps calls himself 'a dull dog' who was prematurely ageing. This expression is alliterative and has an old-fashioned, upper-class sound to it, the kind of expression that a pipe-smoking solicitor would use.**3**

2 Cross-reference to different parts of the text

3 Sophisticated appreciation of language

Kipps appears to be a typically educated middle-class man of his time. He is clearly religious, e.g. 'In answer to my prayer…'.**4** And he has had an effective education as he can recall passages from Shakespeare to match his situation and feelings that he learned at school. The one that came into his memory is the passage from *Hamlet* after Marcellus has seen the ghost of Hamlet's father. This comforts him and helps him to decide to write his story.

4 Aware of religious/spiritual theme

In his early twenties Kipps worked in a London chambers for Mr Bentley. He was young, confident, energetic and impatient so when an opportunity to escape 'the dull details of the conveyancing' arose he welcomed it. He was ambitious in his career and anxious to marry Stella. At this point there had been no suffering in his life that he took for granted. 'My parents were both alive, I had one brother, a good many friends and my fiancée Stella. I was still a young man.' When he hears the background to Alice Drablow's affairs he comments light-heartedly that it is beginning to sound like something from a Victorian novel. This simile suggests amusement as Victorian novels relied heavily on melodrama and were considered old-fashioned and ridiculous.**5**

5 Social/historical understanding

Susan Hill adds depth to the character by the way she integrates comments by the older Kipps on his own behaviour. This is clear in 'The Journey North': Kipps is excited by his task and embarks on his journey to Crythin Gifford with

enthusiasm. He soon becomes tired and although he is reluctant at first to talk to Samuel Daily he wishes to appear important — he folds his newspaper 'with a certain ostentation' as he tries to end the conversation and comments:

'Having in my youthful and priggish way summed up and all but dismissed him…'

Again this emphasises his youth, his arrogance and his inexperience as later Samuel Daily becomes his saviour.**6**

6 Sophisticated interpretation of character

7 Embeds quotations effectively

The landlord of the Gifford Arms receives the same treatment — Kipps confesses 'I had the Londoner's sense of superiority in those days'**7** considering others 'unsophisticated', 'gullible', 'slow-witted' and superstitious. Although the reader could identify with Kipps' youthful exuberance with fondness, his character is balanced as he doesn't seem quite so pleasant here.

It is when the woman in black appears that Kipps gradually begins to change. At first he resists. He does not believe in ghosts. Susan Hill refers to this several times. On his first sighting of the woman in black Kipps is merely curious and quite pleased that Alice Drablow has someone to mourn her after all. He is genuinely kind hearted and sentimental. Her second apparition has a deeper effect; it 'unnerved' him as he began to consider she might be a ghost. The use of the repetition in the past tense suggests that this changed. 'I *did* not believe in ghosts.'**8** That night he had a very disturbed and dreamy *sleep*. From this point in the story he begins to sink into a state of nervous breakdown. 'I felt heavy and sick in the head, stale and tired and jangled too, my nerves and imagination are on edge.'

8 Effective exploration of writer's use of repetition and tense

After several sightings of the lady in black; 'the discovery of the nursery'; the distressing sounds of the child and the pony and trap sinking in the marshes; the final terror — Spider lured by the ghostly whistle into the marshes; these events eventually break down Kipps' resolve to complete his task. When the whole background to the woman in black is revealed to him and he collapses with physical and nervous exhaustion, the reader is in complete sympathy with him and is relieved when Stella arrives to bring him home.

The end happens suddenly and Kipps completes his narrative in a matter-of-fact style which in a strange way makes his experience all the more terrifying. Two years later the woman in black appears once more and robs him of his wife and family.**9**

9 Succinct reference to the plot — not tempted to retell the story

The reader now has insight into the character that Kipps describes himself in the first chapter: the widowed man who, nurtured by Mr Bentley, stayed in the same job all his life and collected watercolours; the 'sombre, pale-complexioned man with a strained expression'. It is not until 13 years after the tragedy that Kipps is sufficiently recovered to marry the widow Esmé and settle for the tranquil life at Monk's Piece intending to retire into the countryside at the first opportunity.

It is in this way that the reader traces the changes in Kipps' character — from the youthful, exuberant and ambitious, carefree young man**10** who persevered through his '...vivid recollections and dreams' into a semi-peaceful existence until he was ready to write his story and face his demons.**11**

10 Sums up character beautifully

11 Effective use of quotation to conclude

What will turn a C-grade essay into an A*-grade essay?

Serious students of English literature will realise there is no foolproof blueprint for this, but there are steps you can take which make achieving an A* grade more likely.

- The first step is to know your text completely and think about all aspects, from the writer's viewpoint to the reader's response.
- The second step is to discuss your ideas about the book with your teacher and fellow students and listen to alternative viewpoints, using this study guide to help you. That way you will realise where you stand on certain issues and how you arrived at your viewpoint.
- Remember to dissect the question. Turn it over in your mind. What do you think the examiner is looking for in your answer?
- Know your Assessment Objectives. Study the mark schemes of sample papers.
- Practise answering questions. Plan your time as well as your content and stick to your plan. A favourite maxim of examiners is to tell students 'to write a lot about a little'. In other words, focus precisely on writer's techniques; the shorter the quotation the better. Then elaborate on your point by giving detailed, in-depth explanation or response.
- Above all, show you have enjoyed the story. It is very difficult to succeed at something you dislike, although conversely, people do come to like what they are good at and consequently succeed. Remember, reading is a pleasure for life, not just for an examination and a ghost story is meant to thrill and chill.

Answers

Answers to *Review your learning* questions.

Context (p. 9)

1 An unmarried mother would not be forced to give up her child in modern times so there would be no story.
2 Very harshly. They were punished severely for any sexual activity outside marriage and were considered either mad or bad.
3 Dickens' *A Christmas Carol* and *The Turn of the Screw* by Henry James.
4 *I'm the King of the Castle*.
5 Six weeks.
6 Stephen Mallatratt.
7 Creating the wide open landscapes and representing the wildlife to create atmosphere.
8 By using Arthur Kipps as narrator, with Kipps employing an actor who encourages him to present the story as a play. In this way, Mallatratt could use Kipps' words to describe the surroundings without elaborate special effects.

Plot and structure (p. 12)

Plot

Chapter 1: Christmas Eve

1 Mr Bentley acts as a father figure to Kipps. He treats him like someone convalescing after an illness or accident. He is anxious to see Kipps settled in a house of his own.
2 Monk's Piece was a handsome, modest house on a grassy knoll at the end of a lane, next to a garden overlooking a meadow. (There was an orchard behind the house.) From one aspect, there was farmland interspersed by woodland and from behind, rough scrub and heath land. It had an air of remoteness and isolation although it was only two miles from the village and seven miles from the nearest market town.
3 Arthur Kipps' state of mind is very fragile particularly when his family starts to tell ghost stories. He is in good general health although he has had occasional nervous illnesses in the past. He seems a rather sombre old man who has to make an effort in company as if to ward off panic attacks. He seems to need solitude in order to cope with his feelings.

Chapter 2: A London Particular

1 'A London Particular' is a colloquial term for a London pea-soup recipe. It is a metaphor for London smog as they are alike in colour and texture.

2 Kipps is a junior solicitor.

3 Alice Drablow was an old eccentric client of Mr Bentley's father. Kipps is sent to represent the firm at her funeral and to begin sorting out her legal affairs.

4 References to the supernatural in this chapter: sense of foreboding; some sixth sense; telepathic intuition; Inferno (hell); ghost figures.

5 Any examples of similes (comparisons using 'like' or 'as'), '...[the fog] was seething through cracks and crannies like sour breath,' creates not just a vivid, visual, image of the fog spreading into every corner but shows the reader how it stank. This helps to build a gloomy picture of early twentieth-century London.

Chapter 3: The Journey North

1 Samuel Daily is in his late fifties, a big man with a beefy face and huge, raw-looking hands; he is well-spoken although has a local accent. He is well-to-do, looks like a prosperous farmer or small business man — *nouveau riche*. He is friendly and hospitable but speaks in a guarded manner especially on the subject of Alice Drablow. He is inquisitive, friendly and plainspoken.

2 Evidence in this chapter that Arthur Kipps is a fairly young, inexperienced man: he is fearful of his new surroundings; he thinks often of his fiancée; he is arrogant, youthful, priggish and makes snap judgements about Samuel Daily; he exaggerates his own importance; he shows off to Samuel Daily; he is talkative.

3 Sea frets are sea mists.

4 The noises of the train adding to the feelings of fear and foreboding: hisses of steam; the huffing of the engine; the clanking of iron; the occasional whistle; the bursts of artillery fire upon the windows; the shriek of the train whistle.

5 The name of the locomotive was 'The Sir Bedivere' which suggests that it was like a strong and trusted warrior. On his deathbed, King Arthur handed over Excalibur to him, his most trusted and strongest warrior, to throw into the lake. In fact, Sir Bedivere was the only one left standing.

Chapter 4: The Funeral of Mrs Drablow

1 In the early twentieth century, Londoners believed that people in the more remote parts of the country were slow and inferior to themselves.

2 Mr Jerome was a land agent whose job was to manage Mrs Drablow's property and sell it after her death.

3 Describe the appearance of the woman in black: see pages 48–49.

4 Kipps was anxious and irritated by the landlord's manner because he felt the landlord was keeping something from him and he wanted to know what it was.

5 Kipps gleaned from the layout of the town that the inhabitants were very inward looking and huddled together for protection from the elements. This is a metaphor for the conspiracy of silence. Nobody will talk about the woman in black, especially not to a stranger.

Chapter 5: Across the Causeway

1 Draw a diagram of EMH and its surrounding as accurately as you can, using the details from pages 60–66. The value of this exercise is solely for you to internalise the atmosphere of isolation and to imagine what Alice Drablow's existence must have been like.

2 This time Arthur Kipps sees the evil in the woman in black. The last time he saw her he felt only sympathy and pity for her.

3 The references to sound accumulate in this chapter:
- Keckwick clucked at the pony
- the marshes lay silent
- the trotting of the pony's hooves
- the rumble of wheels
- harsh weird cries from birds
- smart noise of pony's hooves ceased, to be replaced by hissing, silky sort of sound
- rough scraping of the cart
- faint keening of the wind
- 'rawk rawk' of a hidden bird

They all help build up to an atmosphere of fear and foreboding.

4 Susan Hill suggests the woman in black is a ghost by: her dated costume; extreme pallor and unnaturally bright eyes; the way she moved, slipping between gravestones and through broken gaps in the wall and the way she vanished suddenly.

Chapter 6: The Sound of a Pony and Trap

1 Kipps hears the sound of a pony and trap sinking in the marshes and the screams of its occupants.

2 Kipps is shocked to see Keckwick at 2 a.m. because he believed it was Keckwick driving the pony and trap that he heard sinking earlier.

3 Kipps now firmly believes that the woman in black is a ghost (p. 81); he comes to this realisation by reflecting on the two apparitions and the sounds of the pony and trap sinking.

4 The feeling that this place had changed him and that there was no

going back suggests he is being haunted. 'I did not believe in ghosts' repeats Arthur Kipps on pages 67 and 68. Note the use of the past tense.

Chapter 7: Mr Jerome is Afraid

1 Kipps changes his mind about going back to London as he is affected by the change in the weather and the invigorating bike ride. He returns to his normal equable, cheerful self with no desire to run away. He is going to see the job through.

2 Kipps learns from his visit to Mr Horatio Jerome that nobody but Keckwick is willing to help him sort out Alice Drablow's affairs.

3 Kipps is determined not to be affected by the fear and panic and to get to the bottom of the mystery. He is deliberately trying to be carefree and cheerful.

Chapter 8: Spider

1 Samuel Daily treats Kipps as an uncle would. He lets him make his own decisions even though he disapproves and he is willing to help keep Kipps safe.

2 One possible interpretation is that the landlord treats him with disdain — he ignores him, he doesn't answer his questions and he treats him as though he is a silly young man from London. Another interpretation is that the landlord does not wish to involve himself in Kipps' affairs through fear.

3 Samuel Daily is very proud of his achievements. He is a self-made man, he lives in a grand house, and he is building up his empire for his son and grandson. His speech is simple, direct and this shows he is unashamed of his ambitions. He is astute, up-front and blatantly honest. He is plainly spoken and at times blunt: 'You're a fool if you go on with it'.

Chapter 9: In the Nursery

1 Susan Hill uses Spider the dog to build and relax tension in the story. Spider picks up upon ghostly presences and strange noises outside Kipps' door. She also senses when it is safe before Kipps does.

2 Kipps' bed-time reading is a novel by Walter Scott and John Clare's poetry. This shows he likes adventure and is a romantic.

3 Rose Judd was the governess to Alice Drablow's adopted son.

Chapter 10: Whistle and I'll Come to You

1 Kipps is so physically exhausted and mentally terrified that he passes out on the grass outside the house.

2 He now believes in the power of evil; he believes in ghosts. He has lost his confidence and energy. He has lost his innocence.

3 The isolated house is surrounded by mist. There is a storm outside. The lights go out. There are ghostly noises and both the dog and Kipps are affected by the ghostly presence. There are many apt quotations to support this.

Chapter 11: A Packet of Letters

1 Keckwick's father died on the marshes with the infant son of the woman in black.

2 Mr Jerome is so afraid in Chapter 7 because his child died in suspicious circumstances after one of the appearances of the woman in black.

3 Now Kipps knows the full extent of what the villagers of Crythin Gifford have been keeping from him, he is so deeply traumatised he is physically ill.

Chapter 12: The Woman in Black

1 Any reasonable answer will be rewarded.

2 This question requires a personal response. Any complex feelings that are well supported by textual evidence and explanation will be well rewarded. An honest response is required here. Examiners can recognise answers which have been teacher fed. A 16-year-old's view on any novel will not be the same as a middle-aged person's, as we each bring with us our life experience and we filter what we read through this.

Timeline

Compare your chart with that of a friend and discuss any differences you find.

Structure

Answers speculating on Kipps' life between losing Stella and the Christmas Eve of Chapter 1 should include references to Mr Bentley, changes in Kipps' lifestyle, the development of his career and marriage to Esmé Ainley. The best answers will relate to the profound effect of the haunting by the woman in black and include textual support for points made about character rather than events.

Characterisation (p. 48)

1 Kipps is probably the most successfully presented character in *The Woman in Black*, but any main character is acceptable providing valid reasons are given.

2 Susan Hill makes Kipps interesting by letting us share his responses first hand. She makes us sympathise with him by giving him human faults

which we can recognise in ourselves, like impatience and youthful arrogance.

3 Mr Bentley blames himself for what happens to Kipps because he was his mentor, his employer and he sent him to Crythin Gifford to represent him at Alice Drablow's funeral.

4 Kipps was pleased to see the woman in black at the funeral because he thought she was a personal friend and a genuine mourner.

5 Kipps' reluctance to let Samuel Daily know he travelled to his house for dinner by bicycle shows he is vain and wants to be seen as sophisticated.

6 Arthur Kipps, Jerome, Keckwick, Alice Drablow, Jennet Humfrye or any main character is acceptable as the character with whom the reader has most sympathy providing valid reasons are given.

Themes (p. 54)

1 The voice of the older Kipps enters the narrative to comment on his young self: 'innocence, once lost, is lost for ever'. He means that once you become aware of evil you can never be the same free, uncomplicated person you were before. Knowledge and experience of evil always becomes a burden to the spirit.

2 Juxtaposition means placing alongside, so that the reader can subconsciously measure the contrast between opposites, for example nature and the supernatural, innocence and evil.

Style (p. 64)

1 Susan Hill uses the first-person narrative viewpoint.

2 Examples include the following:
- Metaphor — 'the great cavern of a railway station' is saying that King's Cross Station is an enormous cave.
- Simile — '[the railway station was]…glowing like the interior of a blacksmith's forge'.
- Personification — 'The wind will blow itself out and take the rain with it by the morning,' says Samuel Daily, making the wind and the rain sound like a human couple.

3 Using dialogue helps to create believable characters. The writer can feed information through dialogue to the reader. Dialogue helps break up the text preventing it from becoming dense and monotonous. Dialogue allows the reader to consider the viewpoints of characters other than Kipps.

4 An image creates a picture in the reader's mind and symbolism is an

extension of imagery. A recurring image comes to represent something, for instance black becomes a recognisable symbol of death in this text.

Tackling the exam (p. 70)

1 Separate and embedded quotations.
2 A discourse marker is a word or phrase which links ideas.
3 Keep your introduction short and to the point. Start with a strong statement.
4 A conclusion should draw together all your arguments to a logical finish.
5 It is advisable to adopt an impersonal academic style rather than the very direct style of writing in the first person.

Assessment Objectives and skills (p. 75)

1 When tackling a question:
   - don't retell the story
   - don't try to tell the examiner everything you know
   - don't forget to plan
   - don't run out of time
   - don't use long quotations
   - don't use technical terms without commenting on the effects of the techniques
2 You should read the question carefully and underline the key words.
3 You have 45 minutes to complete your answer; this includes planning and time to check your work.
4 Assessment Objectives are what you should be able to achieve having studied for this exam.
5 You must mention all the key words in the question in the opening paragraph.